On Business and for Pleasure Again

A Self-study Workbook for
Advanced Business English Students

Michael Berman

T0050599

On Business and for Pleasure Again

A Self-study Workbook for Advanced Business English Students

Michael Berman

BOOKS

Winchester, UK
Washington, USA

First published by O-Books, 2011
O-Books is an imprint of John Hunt Publishing Ltd., The Bothy, Deershot Lodge, Park Lane,
Ropley, Hants, SO24 0BE, UK
office1@o-books.net
www.o-books.com

For distributor details and how to order please visit the 'Ordering' section on our website.

Text copyright: Michael Berman 2010

ISBN: 978 1 84694 463 5

A CIP catalogue record for this book is available from the British Library.

Design: Lee Nash

Printed in the UK by CPI Antony Rowe
Printed in the USA by Offset Paperback Mfrs, Inc

We operate a distinctive and ethical publishing philosophy in all
areas of our business, from our global network of authors to
production and worldwide distribution.

CONTENTS

Introduction

Although this workbook, the sequel to *On Business and for Pleasure*, has been designed to help you with your English, it is hoped that the challenges it sets will, at the same time, prove to be enjoyable. An Answer Key has been included so you can check what you have done, and thus work independently, if that is what suits you best. And the exercises are of the kind of length that will enable you to work on them when you have relatively short periods of time to spare, such as while commuting to and from work on public transport. The size of the book should make this convenient too, with it being available in paperback size rather than in a larger format.

You will probably find that working through the material on a regular basis will be of more value than an initial burst of enthusiasm followed by a long lapse. In other words, doing a little on a regular basis is what is recommended rather than attempting to complete everything all in one go, with it going "in one ear and out of the other" so to speak.

Having studied a subject for a very long time, there is a danger of falling into the trap of thinking we know everything there is to know about it. However, there is always more to learn, especially in the case of a living language that is changing all the time. Hopefully, this workbook will go some way towards showing this to be the case.

Working through the material with a good English-English dictionary is to be recommended, ideally one that has been specifically produced for students of English as a Foreign Language, such as the Longmans Dictionary of Contemporary English or the Advanced Learners Dictionary published by Oxford University Press.

I

A Business Parable: Consider the Kind of People You Work With

Place the parts of the story in the correct order:

a. "Ahh," says the beggar, "I have some good news for you. You will find the people in this town are very much the same.

b. "Ahh," says the beggar, "then I have some very bad news for you."

c. "Hello. Can you help me? I am moving to this town. What kind of people live here?" he asks.

d. "Hello. Can you help me? I am moving to this town. What kind of people live here?" he asks.

e. It is at the entry of an old medieval town. There is a blind beggar sitting there as people go about their business. A man enters through the gate and walks up to the beggar.

f. "Let me answer your question with a question. What are the people like in your town?" says the beggar.

g. "Let me answer your question with a question. What are the people like in your town?" says the beggar.

h. The next day, at the same place the same beggar sits. A man enters through the gate and walks up to the beggar.

i. "Well," says the man, "I am going to be happy to be rid of them. Those people are never very nice or helpful. They never have a good word to say and are always looking for favours. You can't trust any of them."

j. "Well," says the man, "that's the problem. The people are all very nice, trustworthy and helpful. They are pleasant and courteous and always willing to lend a hand. We are going to miss them."

1 ___ 2 ___ 3 ___ 4 ___ 5 ___ 6 ___ 7 ___ 8 ___ 9 ___ 10 ___

2

A Business Parable:
Who is Watching You?

No matter what your circumstances are - whether you are a business owner, a professional, or seen as a leader, what you say or do is observed.

Place the parts of the story in the correct order:

a. And, despite his involvement with organized crime, Eddie even tried to teach him right from wrong. Eddie wanted his son to be a better man than he was.

b. Capone had a lawyer nicknamed "Easy Eddie." He was Capone's lawyer for a good reason. Eddie was very good! In fact, Eddie's skill at legal manoeuvring kept Big Al out of jail for a long time.

c. Eddie did have one soft spot, however. He had a son that he loved dearly. Eddie saw to it that his young son had clothes, cars, and a good education. Nothing was withheld. Price was no object.

d. Eddie lived the high life of the Chicago mob and gave little consideration to the atrocity that went on around him.

e. He decided he would go to the authorities and tell the truth about Al "Scarface" Capone, clean up his tarnished name, and offer his son some semblance of integrity. To do this, he would have to testify against The Mob, and he knew that the cost would be great. So, he testified.

f. Many years ago, Al Capone virtually owned Chicago. Capone wasn't famous for anything heroic. He was notorious for enmeshing the windy city in everything from bootlegged booze and prostitution to murder.

g. One day, Easy Eddie reached a difficult decision. Easy Eddie wanted to rectify wrongs he had done.

h. The poem read: *The clock of life is wound but once, and no man has the power to tell just when the hands will stop, at late or early hour. Now is the only time you own. Live, love, toil with a will. Place no faith in time. For the clock may soon be still.*

i. To show his appreciation, Capone paid him very well. Not only was the money big, but Eddie got special dividends, as well. For instance, he and his family occupied a fenced-in mansion with live-in help and all of the conveniences of the day. The estate was so large that it filled an entire Chicago City block.

j. Within the year, Easy Eddie's life ended in a blaze of gunfire on a lonely Chicago Street. But in his eyes, he had given his son the greatest gift he had to offer, at the greatest price he could ever pay. Police removed from his pockets a rosary, a crucifix, a religious medallion, and a poem clipped from a magazine.

k. Yet, with all his wealth and influence, there were two things he couldn't give his son; he couldn't pass on a good name or a good example.

1 ___ 2 ___ 3 ___ 4 ___ 5 ___ 6 ___ 7 ___ 8 ___ 9 ___ 10 ___ 11 ___

3

Phrasal Nouns (i)

From busy airports like Heathrow, planes *take off* every minute or so.

We were informed the *take-off* of our plane would be delayed due to there being snow on the runway.

From the moment I *set out* on the journey, everything seemed to go wrong.

It was clear from the *outset* that this was not going to be my day.

As can be seen from the above examples, phrasal nouns are made from phrasal verbs. Such nouns are often hyphenated, at least early in their history; but there is a strong tendency for such hyphenated forms to evolve into single words. If both versions are current, the hyphenated form is usually the more formal one.

Sometimes the verb is placed first in the formation of the compound noun as in the case of *take-off*, but sometimes it comes second as in the case of *outset*.

As can be seen from the examples below, Latinate nouns tend to be formal whereas phrasal nouns, like phrasal verbs, are more likely to be colloquial and informal: break-up / disintegration, check-up / examination, letdown / disappointment, let-up / relaxation, sell-out / betrayal

Now complete the following sentences with suitable phrasal nouns:

1. The _____ on this face-cream is about 500% so the profit the company is making on each sale is enormous.

[MARK]

2. Unfortunately their disagreement led to a _____ and they are no longer even on speaking terms. [BLOW]

3. If you accept their derisory offer for the company, the result would be a humiliating _____. [BACK]

4. Although the first few workshops attracted a large number of participants, there has unfortunately been a steep _____ in attendance since then. [DROP]

5. The bad annual appraisal my boss gave me was a real _____. [LET]

6. Concerns about the economy triggered a _____ on Wall Street today. [SELL]

7. As there was no way of ever recovering the bad debt, we had no choice but to take a _____ on the loss. [WRITE]

8. We need investors to fund our _____, but unfortunately nobody has shown any interest so far. [START]

9. All you have to do is to choose a password and your _____ will be complete. [LOG]

10. The truth is that instead of being a leader in the field, we're just playing _____ most of the time. [CATCH]

11. It was an insulting remark, a real_____, and not one she is likely to forget in a hurry. [PUT]

12. On paper the candidate looked really impressive, but when we interviewed him, he turned out to be a real _____. [WASH]

4

Phrasal Nouns (ii)

From busy airports like Heathrow, planes *take off* every minute or so.

We were informed the *take-off* of our plane would be delayed due to there being snow on the runway.

From the moment I *set out* on the journey, everything seemed to go wrong.

It was clear from the *outset* that this was not going to be my day.

As can be seen from the above examples, phrasal nouns are made from phrasal verbs. Such nouns are often hyphenated, at least early in their history; but there is a strong tendency for such hyphenated forms to evolve into single words. If both versions are current, the hyphenated form is usually the more formal one.

Sometimes the verb is placed first in the formation of the compound noun as in the case of *take-off*, but sometimes it comes second as in the case of *outset*.

As can be seen from the examples below, Latinate nouns tend to be formal whereas phrasal nouns, like phrasal verbs, are more likely to be colloquial and informal: break-up / disintegration, check-up / examination, letdown / disappointment, let-up / relaxation, sell-out / betrayal

Now complete the following sentences with suitable phrasal nouns:

1. If you don't want to use a password to secure your laptop, that's your _____, but it's not to be recommended.

[LOOK]

2. What this company needs is a complete _____ because the way it is currently being run is a recipe for disaster. [SHAKE]

3. What is attractive about the scheme is that for a small initial _____, an enormous profit can be made. [LAY]

4. The _____ in negotiations between the two sides, just as they finally seemed to be getting somewhere, is really most frustrating. [BREAK]

5. Now there is a real possibility that the bank could fail, the only solution to the problem would seem to be a government _____. [BAIL]

6. An _____ in the economy is what we are all hoping for as it should lead to the creation of new jobs. [TURN]

7. The loss of the government subsidy was a _____ to the company's expansion plans. [SET]

8. What the _____ of the talks will be is still unclear, but we remain optimistic. [COME]

9. If any further _____ are announced, the effect on the morale of the staff will be devastating. [LAY]

10. I only wish there was more I could do, but until I am finally given the _____, I am afraid my hands are tied. [GO]

11. Everything about the product seems to be perfect. The only _____ is the price. [DRAW]

12. It is high time we had a _____ on such practices within the company as they cause a great deal of ill-feeling. [CRACK]

Phrasal Nouns (iii)

From busy airports like Heathrow, planes *take off* every minute or so.

We were informed the *take-off* of our plane would be delayed due to there being snow on the runway.

From the moment I *set out* on the journey, everything seemed to go wrong.

It was clear from the *outset* that this was not going to be my day.

As can be seen from the above examples, phrasal nouns are made from phrasal verbs. Such nouns are often hyphenated, at least early in their history; but there is a strong tendency for such hyphenated forms to evolve into single words. If both versions are current, the hyphenated form is usually the more formal one.

Sometimes the verb is placed first in the formation of the compound noun as in the case of *take-off*, but sometimes it comes second as in the case of *outset*.

As can be seen from the examples below, Latinate nouns tend to be formal whereas phrasal nouns, like phrasal verbs, are more likely to be colloquial and informal: break-up / disintegration, check-up / examination, letdown / disappointment, let-up / relaxation, sell-out / betrayal

Now complete the following sentences with suitable phrasal nouns:

1. The _____ we receive in response to the questionnaire will help us to provide a better service. [FEED]

2. The _____ will come into effect almost immediately, and the effect should be more or less instantaneous. [CHANGE]

3. The enticing offer was just a _____, an attempt to attract new customers into the shop. [COME]

4. I was hoping we would be able to come to some kind of agreement, but all she did was to give me the _____. [RUN]

5. The government _____ will have a serious impact on the NHS, and are likely to lead to longer waiting lists. [CUT]

6. His pretence of indifference was just a _____, and underneath the surface he was actually extremely hurt by the criticism he faced. [PUT]

7. To put forward the excuse that you are too busy to attend the meeting is just a _____ because everyone knows that is not the case. [COP]

8. Nobody likes being given the _____ and I am no different to anyone else in that respect. [BRUSH]

9. The _____ of the hall where the Conference is being held is far from ideal for the purpose and we need to adapt it somehow before the event takes place. [LAY]

10. The _____ of the old model is just about complete and the time has now come to launch the new version. [PHASE]

11. I accept there has been a bit of a _____ over the arrangements and I am sorry about that, but in no way can I be held to blame as I was not even on duty at the time. [MIX]

12. To help pay for the _____ of the palace, it will be opened to the public for nine months every year and visitors will have to pay an admission fee. [KEEP]

6

Phrasal Adjectives

Not only can phrasal nouns be formed from phrasal verbs, there are also phrasal adjectives.

Such adjectives are often hyphenated, at least early in their history; but there is a strong tendency for such hyphenated forms to evolve into single words. If both versions are current, the hyphenated form is usually the more formal one.

Now complete the following sentences with suitable phrasal adjectives:

1. Nothing happened the way we expected it to so it was lucky we had a _____ plan. [BACK]
2. After a long day at work, neither of us felt like cooking so we ordered a _____ [TAKE] meal
3. There are no seats left on the last flight to Paris but you might be able to get a _____ ticket. [STAND]
4. _____ luggage has to be stored in the overhead lock above your seat. [CARRY]
5. At the Annual General Meeting, the shareholders voted to reject the _____ bid so the company will not become swallowed up by a multi-national, as was the fear, and will continue instead to remain independent. [TAKE]
6. The _____ procedure at the airport has become automated so the long queues that used to form at the desks are now a thing of the past. [CHECK]
7. In case your offer is rejected, you need to make sure you have a _____ position. [FALL]
8. Whatever you decide today, does not have to be final;

there is a fourteen day _____ period built into the contract in case you want to change your mind. [COOL]

9. I wonder why there is such a high staff _____ rate in the company, and why nobody stays there for any length of time. [TURN]

10. Although people are constantly joining the Health Club, most only attend for a month or so, and the _____ rate is high. [DROP]

11. Before you start your _____ in the gym, you need to do some warm-up exercises first. [WORK]

12. A well-_____ plan like the one you came up with has every chance of success. [THINK]

13. The _____ theory, which suggests that poor people benefit when richer people become even richer, is just a fallacy. [TRICKLE]

14. Since you are clearly not happy about the way the Party is being run, perhaps you should consider forming a _____ group. [BREAK]

15. It is a highly _____ job and should attract a large number of applicants. [SEEK]

7

How to Write a Business Plan
(Word Formation)

For each gap, use the given root word to make the correct form of the missing word:

The business plan captures the 1 _____ [strategy] operational and 2 _____ [finance] aims of the business. A good business plan will contain an introduction _____ [summary] the detail of the proposal, a written 4 _____ [view] of the business' aims, its product or service, details of the 5 _____ [manage] team, and financial forecasts and appendices.

Explain what your business will do in simple terms, 6 _____ [light] any features that set it apart from rivals. 7 _____ [line] what part of the market you are targeting, key 8 _____ [compete] and what 9 _____ [differ] you from them.

Details of key 10 _____ [person] and their relevant experience are also important, as is 11 _____ [operate] 12 _____ [inform] like office 13 _____ [locate], special 14 _____ [equip] and expected employee 15 _____ [count].

As well as stating the financing you need, your plan should also include a sales forecast, 16 _____ [cash] forecast and a projected profit and loss account. The figures used must be 17 _____ [reason] - avoid being over 18 _____

[optimist] and employ a qualified 19 _____ [account] to
make sure there are no 20 _____ [slip] along the way.

Small Firms and the Problem
of Late Payments (Word Formation)

For each gap, use the given root word to make the correct form of the missing word:

More small and medium-sized businesses are suffering 1 _____ [hard] as their customers make late payments, 2 _____ [search] suggests.

Late payments are a problem for all firms because they disrupt their 3 _____ [flow]. If payments do not arrive on time, they have to use their own funds to cover the delay, or go to their banks to try and extend 4 _____ [draft]. It also forces them to invest time and 5 _____ [source] on chasing payments.

It is an even bigger problem for small businesses, though, as when a small firm is paid late, it is forced to go to the bank, and when banks are not loaning or giving overdrafts, it means small firms feel like banks themselves. Large firms are 6 _____ [prove] their cash flow on the back of smaller suppliers. If only large, blue-chip firms were more 7 _____ [ethics] and paid on time, there would be no problem but 8 _____ [fortune], being 9 _____ [real], there is little 10 _____ [likely] of this.

11 _____ [withstand] the fact that bad debts and late payment of invoices are endemic problems for UK businesses, there are actually 12 _____ [serve] offered by banks to help companies

in such circumstances. What causes concern, though, is that so few small firms are aware or making use, of these 13 _____ [alter].

Despite the fact that most firms have payment terms that include a 14 _____ [line], 15 _____ [force] it is another matter. Companies do have a legal right to demand interest on unpaid bills, but in practice they rarely get it and taking legal 16 _____ [act] to 17 _____ [cover] such interest is not 18 _____ [usual] a viable option due to the 19 _____ [proportion] and, most would say, 20 _____ [reason] costs involved.

How to Start Working from Home
(Word Formation)

For each gap, use the given root word to make the correct form of the missing word:

The benefits of working from home are tangible. No 1 _____ [night] journeys on 2 _____ [commute] trains or 3 _____ [grid] on motorway, plus the 4 _____ [able] to stroll out into your own garden 5 _____ [when] you fancy a 10-minute break.

But you need to be disciplined, organised and have access to the right technical 6 _____ [equip]. If things go wrong it can be very lonely and 7 _____ [depress] stuck inside on your own with only the cat for company on dark winter evenings.

The internet is perhaps the single most important 8 _____ [fact] behind people being able to work from home. You must 9 _____ [sure], 10 _____ [how], that what you have is 11 _____ [rely] otherwise it will irritate both you and your clients and cause you a great deal of 12 _____ [frustrate].

Your internet 13 _____ [connect] is vital. There are many different internet service providers and personal 14 _____ [recommend] can be 15 _____ [value] when you are trying to make a choice.

Take advantage of the free 16 _____ [introduce] offers many companies now offer but check that there are no 17 _____ [hide] charges. Scrutinise the 18 _____ [agree] and make sure you cancel before the 19 _____ [line] if you don't want to end up paying a month's 20 _____ [subscribe] unnecessarily.

Payment Fraud (Word Formation)

For each gap, use the given root word to make the correct form of the missing word:

Fraudsters are stepping up their efforts to steal money from our bank accounts. As our 1 _____ [pay] methods continue to change, so 2 _____ [artist] will find new ways to trick people out of their money. Fraudsters have found clever ways of circumventing some new card technology, but they need to be 3 _____ [extreme] well-organised to do so. 4 _____ [innovate] does not 5 _____ [automate] cause an increase in fraud, although fraudsters are generally 6 _____ [speak] quicker to adapt to changing systems than 7 _____ [consume].

Phishing attacks are on the increase - when fraudsters trick people out of their bank account details using bogus e-mails - or by using malicious 8 _____ [ware] that tracks what users typed to gather 9 _____ [word] and credit card numbers.

There are always risks if you are not 10 _____ [care] with your cards or your 11 _____ [person] 12 _____ [inform], but cash has its dangers as well. 13 _____ [pocket] and thieves still operate and it is never a good idea to carry around large amounts of cash or keep big sums hidden at home. Always shield the 14 _____ [pad] and make sure the cash is securely in a wallet or purse when using a 15 _____ [cash].

Some basic advice includes not letting your cards or your card details out of your sight when making a 16 _____[transact], not keeping your 17 _____ [word], 18 _____ [log] details or Pins written down, and not 19 _____ [disclose] Pins, login details or passwords in response to 20 _____ [solicit] emails.

Never enter your card details on a 21 _____ [site] you have accessed via a link from an e-mail. 22 _____ [sure] you shop at secure websites by checking that the security icon is showing in your browser window. Always log out after shopping and save the 23 _____ [confirm] e-mail as a record of your purchase

Anyone who is a victim of fraud is not liable and, as long as you have not acted 24 _____ [fraud] or without 25 _____ [reason] care, you will be reimbursed if somebody uses your card, steals it, or clones it.

Irresponsible Lending Prohibited (Word Formation)

For each gap, use the given root word to make the correct form of the missing word:

1 _____ [lend] have been told they must not 2 _____ [lead] borrowers and must assess if customers can afford to 3 _____ [pay] loans. The 4 _____ [require] form part of new 5 _____ [guide] from the Office of Fair Trading (OFT) to 6 _____ [act] 7 _____ [response] lending, and all consumer credit businesses are expected to fully comply with both the word and spirit of this new set of 8 _____ [guide].

The new measures are designed to help to protect consumers and 9 _____ [able] the OFT to clamp down on 10 _____ [scruple] lenders who lure people into taking on loans they cannot afford. A prime example is the common practice of showering borrowers with offers of new credit cards, with minimal checks on individuals' 11 _____ [credit].

What is stipulated is that companies should not use 12 _____ [lead] or 13 _____ [oppress] 14 _____ [behave] when advertising, selling, or 15 _____ [force] a credit 16 _____ [agree], and that they should make a 17 _____ [reason] 18 _____ [assess] of what a borrower can afford to manage. 19 _____ [add], lenders are expected to clearly explain to the borrowers what, under the terms of the contract, their 20 _____ [commit] will be, so there can be no 21 _____ [understand] and an informed choice can thus be made.

The focus on getting firms' practices and 22 _____ [proceed] right is a big step towards 23 _____ [sure] consumers are treated fairly and not 24 _____ [courage] into taking out 25 _____ [afford] and 26 _____ [sustain] credit that lands them even deeper in debt.

A Letter in Application for a Job

From each set of alternatives, select the most appropriate choice of wording for a formal letter in application for a job. Sometimes more than one option might be acceptable, and sometimes perhaps none of them will be:

1.

a. Your address, contact numbers, e-mail, and the date on the left side of the page, followed by the name, department, and address of the person you are writing to.

b. Your address, contact numbers, e-mail, and the date on the right side of the page, followed by the name, department, and address of the person you are writing to.

c. The name, department, and address of the person you are writing to on the left side of the page, followed by your address, contact numbers, e-mail, and the date.

d. The name, department, and address of the person you are writing to on the right side of the page, followed by your address, contact numbers, e-mail, and the date.

Dear sir / madam,

2.

a. How are you doing?

b. Hope you're well.

c. I trust this letter finds you in good health.

d. How's it going?

e. I hope you're well and enjoying life.

f. _____ (no greeting necessary)

3.

a. I am writing this letter to apply for the position of _____ that I saw advertised on your website.

b. I am interested in the position of _____ that was advertised in this week's edition of _____.

c. I'm writing to apply for the job of _____ that I saw advertised in my local newspaper.

d. A friend of mine told me you're looking for a _____, and that's why I decided to get in touch.

4.

a. I'm really keen on a career with your organization because of your excellent reputation as _____.

b. All I can say is give me the job and you can be sure you won't regret it

c. I am particularly interested in a career with your organization because of your excellent reputation as _____.

d. To be honest, I'm desperate for a job and I'd be prepared to do absolutely anything if it meant having some money at last.

e. I'm particularly interested in a career with your organization because I've been told you pay more than anyone else.

I graduated from _____ in _____, where I received high grades in both _____ and _____. In addition, I have an EU passport, an international driving licence and I am also fully computer literate.

Over the past two years I have worked in _____, helping to _____, and I can safely say this experience has given me the ability to deal

5.

a. with even the most awkward clients

b. with all sorts, even complete idiots.

c. with the needs of all types of people.

d. with people from all walks of life.

e. with absolutely anybody, even total dickheads.

6.

a. It is my firm belief that I can offer

b. I'm one hundred and one per cent certain I can offer

c. I've got absolutely no doubt at all that I can offer

d. Hopefully, I should be able to offer

e. With a bit of luck I should be able to offer

f. If everything works out all right, I should be able to offer

g. I am confident I can offer

... your company strong interpersonal skills, organizational ability, and considerable previous experience in the field and, for these reasons, I believe I would be a valuable addition to your team.

7.

a. As requested, together with this covering letter, I am enclosing my resume for your review. And I hope you will give me the opportunity to meet and share more about my qualifications and the ways in which I can contribute to your company.

b. As requested, together with this covering letter, I am enclosing a copy of my CV. And I hope you will give me the opportunity to meet and share more about my qualifications and the ways in which I can contribute to your company.

8.

a. Looking forward to hearing from you.

b. Thank you for your consideration.

c. I trust that you will give this matter your urgent attention.

d. I look forward to hearing from you.

e. Please let me know if you are interested as soon as possible.

9.

a. Yours sincerely,

b. Yours faithfully,

c. Kind regards,

d. Wishing you all the best,

e. Best wishes,

13

A Letter of Complaint

From each set of alternatives, select the most appropriate choice of wording for a formal letter of complaint. Sometimes more than one option might be acceptable, and sometimes perhaps none of them will be:

Dear sir / madam,

1.
a. How are you doing?
b. Hope you're well.
c. I trust this letter finds you in good health.
d. How's it going?
e. I hope you're well and enjoying life.
f. _____ (no greeting necessary)

2.
a. I am writing is to let you know how dissatisfied I am with _____

b. I am writing to say how concerned / upset I am about _____

c. I am contacting you to express my disappointment with _____

d. I'm really pissed off with _____
e. I can't tell you how fed up I am with _____
f. I'm sick and tired of _____
g. I am writing to complain in the strongest possible terms about _____

h. I'm writing to complain as strongly as I can about

_____

3.

a. the poor service that I have received from your company.

b. the rubbish service you provide.

c. how awful your service is.

d. all the problems we've had with your company.

e. all the problems you've caused us.

The reason why we chose you rather than any of your competitors is because you promise on the front page of your website, and also in your brochure, to deal with problems both quickly and efficiently.

4.

a. But in fact it's all a pack of lies.

b. But what a load of lies that turned out to be.

c. However, the reality is you do nothing of the sort.

d. But all you've done is to mess us around.

e. So why haven't you done so is what I want to know.

5.

a. What was particularly annoying was the way you _____ as this meant we were unable to _____

b. The main problem was that you failed to provide me with _____ and this meant I was unable to _____

c. What really pissed me off was the way you _____ which meant I wasn't able to _____

d. The main problem was that you didn't provide me with _____ which meant I had to _____.

e. What really inconvenienced us was the way you _____ as this meant our clients were unable to ____

6.

a. So what the hell are you going to do about it?

b. Not surprisingly, what I / we would now like to know what you intend to do about this.

c. Consequently, what I / we need to know now is how you plan to rectify this.

d. I / We now need to know what you plan to do about this.

e. As a result, we feel the least you can do is to offer us some form of compensation.

7.

a. And you'd better reply to this or else!

b. Thank you for your consideration.

c. I trust that you will give this matter your urgent attention.

d. I look forward to hearing from you.

e. I would appreciate it if this situation could be resolved as soon as possible.

8.

a. Yours sincerely,

b. Yours faithfully,

c. Kind regards,

d. Wishing you all the best,

e. Best wishes,

14

A Letter Responding to a Complaint

From each set of alternatives, select the most appropriate choice of wording for a formal letter responding to a complaint. Sometimes more than one option might be acceptable, and sometimes perhaps none of them will be:

1.
a. Your address, contact numbers, e-mail, and the date on the left side of the page, followed by the name, department, and address of the person you are writing to.
b. Your address, contact numbers, e-mail, and the date on the right side of the page, followed by the name, department, and address of the person you are writing to.
c. The name, department, and address of the person you are writing to on the left side of the page, followed by your address, contact numbers, e-mail, and the date.
d. The name, department, and address of the person you are writing to on the right side of the page, followed by your address, contact numbers, e-mail, and the date.

Dear sir / madam,

2.
a. How are you doing?
b. Hope you're well.
c. I trust this letter finds you in good health.
d. How's it going?
e. I hope you're well and enjoying life.
f. _____ (no greeting necessary)

3.

a. I was most concerned to receive your letter regarding your complaint. I can fully understand the distress this must have caused and I can assure you that we will conduct a full investigation into what took place.

b. Sorry to read you're so upset, but not sure there's much I can do about it.

c. I would like to apologise from the bottom of my heart for the manner in which you have been treated, and I can assure you that the person responsible will be reprimanded most severely.

d. I was extremely upset to read that you are not satisfied with the service you have received and I can assure you a full investigation will be conducted into what happened.

e. A thousand apologies for the mess we've made of things. And I can understand the way you must be feeling because I'd be furious if I'd been treated that way too.

4.

a. If what you write is true, then the level of service you received was clearly unacceptable and I owe you an apology.

b. But there are two sides to every story, as I'm sure you know, and I need to speak to the member of staff concerned to find out whether you're telling the truth or not before doing anything else.

c. There can be no excuse for a lackadaisical attitude on the part of any of our employees, and we take such matters extremely seriously.

d. The company aims to consistently deliver a professional service to our customers, but on this occasion it would seem we have failed, so please accept my apologies.

5.

a. Thank you for giving us the opportunity to assist you, and once our investigations are complete, we will of course contact you about our findings.

b. Thanks for letting us know about it, and sorry once again.

c. Thank you again for your comments and we hope that you will be willing to give us another chance to serve you once we have resolved this issue.

d. Thank you for bringing this matter to my attention and we hope that you will have no further cause for any complaint in relation to our service.

e. The company is actively working to improve service levels and your feedback has proved to be invaluable. So thank you for taking the time to bring the matter to our attention and, as a goodwill gesture, we would like to offer you a 50% discount off your next order with the firm.

6.

a. And if there's anything else you can think of that we can do to help, just drop us a line.

b. That's all for now.

c.   In the meantime, if we can be of any further help, please let us know.

d. Have a good day.

7.

a. Yours sincerely,

b. Yours faithfully,

c. Kind regards,

d. Wishing you all the best,

e. Best wishes,

A Letter to Find Out More Information About a Product

From each set of alternatives, select the most appropriate choice of wording for a formal letter written to find out more information about a product. Sometimes more than one option might be acceptable, and sometimes perhaps none of them will be:

1.
a. The name, address, and phone number of the person you are writing to on the left hand side of the page.
b. Your name, address, and phone number on the left hand side of the page.
c. The name, address, and phone number of the person you are writing to on the left hand side of the page, followed by your name, address, and phone number.
d. Your name, address, and phone number on the left hand side of the page, followed by the name, address, and phone number of the person you are writing to.

2.
a. Date
b. No date required as it will be on the postmark

3.
a. Dear Mr. _____, Mrs. _____, or Ms. _____,
b. Hello!
c. How are you?
d. Dear sir/madam,
e. Esteemed sirs,

f. To whom it may concern:

4.

a. This is a request for information about _____

b. I am interested in _____ that was advertised _____

c. I'd like to know more about _____ what was featured _____

d. I want to know about _____ that I saw advertised _____

e. I would like more information about _____ that was featured _____

f. Please tell me more about _____ what was advertised _____

g. I'm writing because I've got a problem. I need to know more about _____

5.

a. Judging from the advert, the product would seem to be ideal.

b. Based on the information in the advert, the product would suit my needs perfectly.

c. If the advert is to be believed, it seems to be a real bargain.

d. With a bit of luck, it might be just what I've been looking for.

e. I've been trying to get hold of one of these for ages now, so when I saw your advert my eyes nearly popped right out of my head!

6.

a. But I'm still not sure to be honest with you.

b. However, to be honest with you, it all seems a bit too good to be true.

c. But I need to be 100% sure before I go ahead and buy it.

d. However, how can I be sure you're not trying to trick me?

e. But money doesn't grow on trees, you know.

7.

a. That's why I need to know _____
b. For this reason it would be useful if you could tell me _____
c. That is why it would be helpful to know _____
d. So sorry to be a nuisance, but I have to ask _____
e. So don't give me any bullshit and just tell me straight: _____ ?

8.

a. It would also be helpful if you could tell me_____
b. One more thing I need to know is _____
c. It would also be appreciated if you could tell me _____
d. Another thing I need to know is _____
e. It would also be helpful if you could let me know _____

9.

a. And last but not least, details of _____ would be a help too.
b. Finally, and perhaps most important of all, we also need to know _____
c. And one more thing too, before it slips my mind. I want to know _____
d. Additionally, some more details about _____ would assist us enormously too.

10.

a. If I don't report back with this information quickly, my boss is going to murder me so please don't let me down.
b. I would be grateful if you could provide me with this information as soon as possible please.
c. Thank you in advance for your cooperation.
d. Thanks a lot for helping me out.
e. Please answer this quickly and don't mess me around.
f. A quick response would be very much appreciated as time

is of the essence.

g. A quick response would be very much appreciated as I'm a busy man and don't take kindly to being made to wait for things.

11.

a. Sincerely,

b. Yours sincerely

c. Faithfully,

d. Yours faithfully,

e. Your obedient servant

f. With all good wishes

g. I remain, as always, yours truly

h. All the best,

12.

a. PS 'Sorry about the recycled envelope, but I didn't have any new ones left and all the shops were closed.

b. I would like to apologize for posting this to you in a recycled envelope. Unfortunately, due to an administrative error, we ran out of new ones and, under the circumstances, it was the only way to ensure the letter reached you quickly.

c. PS. 'Sorry about the recycled envelope, but we're into saving trees in our office – one of my boss's bright ideas!

16

Phrasal Verbs with INTO

INTO indicates involvement or some kind of transformation, sometimes with positive and sometimes with negative results. All the sentences below contain phrasal verbs with INTO. Your job is to find the missing verbs:

1. You have _____ the company into a real success and you should be extremely proud of what you have achieved.
2. It's a frightening experience _____ into the unknown, but something we all have to face at some point in our lives.
3. We had a lot of problems initially but eventually everything _____ into place.
4. If you have the time, I would be grateful if you could _____ into the possibility for me.
5. She _____ into him purely by chance when she was at the Conference last week.
6. If you agree to what they are suggesting it would be a big mistake, because you would be _____ right into their hands.
7. If we lower the price of the product, I am afraid it is going to _____ into our profits.
8. The company _____ into something much larger than either of us had ever expected when we first set it up.
9. As much as I would like to be able to help you, I think it would be extremely risky to _____ into such a scheme.
10. The truth is that you are in a real mess and the best advice I can give you is to _____ into a rehab clinic.
11. I wonder what the current exchange rate is as I would like to _____ these dollars into pounds.

12. He _____ away all the money he inherited from his father so now he has to start again from scratch.

13. I wish I knew how we could _____ into the market but the truth is I have no idea at all.

14. You really _____ into your boss at the meeting so it is hardly surprising he reacted the way that he did, and you can count yourself lucky that you still have a job.

15. To _____ into someone's computer you need to know their password, and you might then be able to access their bank accounts.

17

Phrasal Verbs with AWAY

When you are AWAY you are in a sense no longer present, physically or mentally. All the sentences below contain phrasal verbs with AWAY. Your job is to find the missing verbs:

1. I really feel I need to _____ away even if it is only for a day or two.
2. We are selling the products so cheaply that we are more or less _____ them away.
3. I am delighted to say I _____ away from the workshop with a new found sense of purpose.
4. Nobody should ever be _____ away as we should be able to find a place for everyone who comes to us for help.
5. I know it is a difficult task you have set yourself, but if you keep _____ away at it, I'm sure you will get there in the end.
6. Please _____ away and do not come back because I never want to see you again as long as I live.
7. I wish we could somehow _____ away all this negativity because it is creating a really bad atmosphere in the office.
8. We warned them to _____ away but unfortunately they did not listen and now they are paying the price.
9. A relaxing massage in the hotel spa would soon _____ away all your aches and pains.
10. I wish there were some positives we could _____ away from the meeting but it is all looking rather bleak.
11. Wasting your time _____ your life away is not going to do you much good. When are you going to stop messing

around and find yourself a proper job?

12. He _____ into a large sum of money when his father died and used it to do what he had always dreamt of - to start up a business of his own.

13. She _____ away from giving a straight answer to the question in the interview as she did not want to commit herself.

14. I have no idea why he _____ away in the way that he did, I suppose he did not want anyone to notice that he was leaving early

15. Instead of _____ your money away betting on horses, you would be better off investing it in a savings account.

18

Phrasal Verbs with OVER

When you are OVER something or someone, you view things from a different angle and you enter into a new relationship with that person or thing. All the sentences below contain phrasal verbs with OVER. Your job is to find the missing verbs:

1. It took me a long time to _____ over the disappointment of being overlooked for promotion, but now I have come to terms with it.
2. I would like you to _____ over these figures once again please to make sure that I have not made any mistakes.
3. At first my colleagues were reluctant to accept the changes I had proposed, but eventually I managed to _____ them over.
4. At first I thought you _____ over as being quite arrogant, but then I realised I had misjudged you.
5. Please _____ it over and I am sure you will agree in the end that it is really our only option.
6. As we did not have enough time to discuss everything at our meeting today, I have arranged to delay my flight and to _____ over for another night.
7. I know we have had our differences in the past but it is time we _____ over a new leaf and learnt to work together.
8. I am finding it impossible to work this way with you _____ over me all the time.
9. If you want them to agree to your proposal, you need to _____ it over more clearly.
10. You clearly have no idea how to use the machine, so

_____ over and let me have a go.

11. Once all this waiting _____ over it will be a great relief to all of us.

12. If you think you can just _____ all over me, then you are in for a nasty shock.

13. The first thing we plan to do when we _____ over the company is to negotiate new contracts with everyone.

14. I am afraid we seem to have run out of time, so we will have to _____ over the remaining points for discussion on the list until next week's meeting.

15. Despite the fact that I spent hours _____ over the document, I could not make head or tail of it.

19

Phrasal Verbs with OUT

If we are IN the dark or OUT of the light, we have a problem that needs solving. All the sentences below contain phrasal verbs with OUT. Your job is to find the missing verbs:

1. It took me ages to _____ out a solution to the problem as it was not one I had come across before.
2. Actually, he was planning to sell the company, but we managed to _____ him out of it in the end.
3. I cannot possibly cover all the points, but I will attempt to _____ out and deal with some of the most important ones.
4. Although she dislikes her new job intensely, she has no choice but to _____ it out, at least until she can find something better.
5. I imagine it must be a very painful memory for you so it is not surprising you do your best to _____ it out. But perhaps it would be more helpful if you could talk about it to someone.
6. Having to deal with bureaucracy _____out the very worst in me I'm afraid to say.
7. I wonder what you are hoping to _____out of this Conference. As with all such events, I imagine it will depend to a large extent on what you are prepared to put into it.
8. We need to _____out sexism in the workplace once and for all as it is totally unacceptable in this day and age.
9. I think the only solution is for you to _____ out permanently and to take all your belongings with you this time.
10. I hope to _____out and join you just as soon as I possibly

can, but problems at work mean that I will not be able to for the time being.

11. If you do a search on the Internet, you will _____out that the company does not actually exist.

12. Unfortunately we _____out with each other we are no longer even on speaking terms.

13. When you _____out on a journey, you can never tell exactly what it will ultimately lead to, and that is what makes it so exciting.

14. There has not been much demand for that particular course so we have decided to _____ it out of the training programme in future and to replace it with an alternative option.

15. I could not _____out what you were saying when I phoned you from my mobile because your voice kept breaking up.

20

Does Money Make You Happy?
(Use of the Articles)

Fill in the gaps in the following passage with a(n) or the. Leave gaps empty if no article is required:

1 ___ unhappy answer to whether or not your happiness expands in 2 ___ line with your wealth is "yes, but - no, but". It seems it does if your riches rise relative to that of 3 ___ Joneses, but not if you all rise together. Studies show that what we actually care about is our income compared with 4 ___ other people. But if over time everybody is becoming richer then people don't on 5 ___ average feel any better than they did before.

What we find is 6 ___ paradox. 7 ___ apparent contradiction is that people in 8 ___ richer countries don't seem to be any happier now than they were previously despite their enrichment through economic growth, but that people who are richer at any one time are happier on 9 ___ average than people who are poorer. And 10 ___ conclusion to be drawn is that happiness depends on relative incomes and wealth.

This is partly because aspirations rise with 11 ___ incomes. As 12 ___ people tend to adapt quickly to having more money, they do not get 13 ___ pleasure out of it that they expected to get. People's aspirations tend to rise as their incomes rise, so rather quickly they start to think of 14 ___ lot of additional things that they need to buy, and they end up no happier than they were before.

It is true that 15 ___ richer people are, by and large happier than their poorer neighbours, but it is not necessarily 16 ___ money that brings this about. It may be that richer people are more likely to hold jobs in which people defer to them or they have more autonomy in what they do. So it does not always follow that giving more money, if you don't change those other things, is really going to make much of 17 ___ difference.

So if 18 ___ money is not all it is cracked up to be, then what should 19 ___ people and governments do? What is clear is that 20 ___ break-neck chase after 21 ___ economic growth is misplaced, and that this competition to get richer than other people cannot be achieved at 22 ___ level of 23 ___ society. Perhaps what we should focus on instead is trying to increase 24 ___ total amount of happiness, which means enabling 25 ___ people to have better human relationships.

21

The End of the Cheque
(Use of the Articles)

Fill in the gaps in the following passage with a(n) or the. Leave gaps empty if no article is required:

Consumers in 1 ___ UK should expect 2 ___ revolution in 3 ___ way they pay for things in 4 ___ near future. This is because 5 ___ cheque is said to be in 6 ___ irreversible decline as 7 ___ innovation points towards 8 ___ cashless society.

9 ___ chip can be placed in 10 ___ everyday item such as 11 ___ mobile phone. This is then pushed against 12 ___ sensor in 13 ___ shop to pay, and is known as 14 ___ "contactless" technology.

15 ___ earliest cheque in 16 ___ UK was thought to have been written about 350 years ago, dated 16 February. It was made out for £400, signed by Nicholas Vanacker, made payable to 17 ___ Mr Delboe, and drawn on Messrs Morris and Clayton - scriveners and bankers of 18 ___ City of London.

19___ cheque's predecessor was 20 ___ bill of exchange – 21 ___ way for traders to buy and sell 22 ___ goods without 23 ___ need to carry cumbersome and valuable quantities of gold and silver.

In 24 ___ early days, cheques were used relatively infrequently, mainly by 25 ___ merchants and traders for high-value transactions. They had to be confident that these handwritten pieces of paper could be guaranteed. So they were often issued by goldsmiths within 26 ___ local network of traders who knew and trusted each other. Printing processes meant they started to be used by customers of commercial banks, peaking in 27 ___ 1990s.

As well as electronic transfer of funds on 28 ___ internet, 29 ___ most likely replacement for 30 ___ cheque is mobile payments. 31 ___ phone number acts as 32 ___ proxy for 33 ___ bank account number. So instead of paying, for example, 34 ___ plumber by cheque - he or she could be paid by 35 ___ exchange of text messages.

22

Verbs Followed by the Gerund or the Infinitive

Certain verbs can be followed by the Gerund or the Infinitive, but with a change of meaning. For example, MEAN followed by the Gerund is a synonym for ENTAIL whereas MEAN followed by the Infinitive with TO is a synonym for INTEND. Look at these examples:

> If the only way to save the company means cutting back on staff, then I'm afraid that's what we'll have to do.
> Where do you mean to hold the meeting – in your office or in a neutral location?

Now match the numbers below with the letters to complete the sentences. The first has been done for you:

1. **Do you like**
2. Due to recent political unrest, the Foreign Office advises
3. I forget
4. I've noticed some mistakes in the report and it needs
5. If you go on
6. If you need
7. If you stop
8. I kept meaning
9. I know you're trying
10. In view of the serious nature of the situation drastic measures are called for, which means
11. I remember
12. I wouldn't like

13. Make sure you don't forget
14. Now that you have finished this particular project, what are you going on
15. Now that you know all the facts, I suppose you regret
16. Please remember
17. Please stop
18. We regret
19. We strongly advise you
20. We tried

a. against travelling to the country at present.
b. **being self-employed or would you prefer to work for a company?**
c. checking before it is ready to be submitted.
d. closing this branch I'm afraid.
e. discussing it at our last meeting, but I don't believe we came to any conclusions.
f. having discussed it with you before, but I suppose I must have done.
g. having made the decision that you did.
h. lowering prices in an attempt to increase sales but unfortunately it made little difference.
i. telling me what to do all the time. It's getting on my nerves.
j. to consider the possible consequences I'm sure you'll agree that it's just not worth the risk.
k. to do next?
l. to go freelance as I prefer the security of a regular full-time job.
m. to inform you we have no vacancies at present but will keep your CV on file in case something does come up.
n. to make any changes, please do not do so without consulting me first..
o. to send the report to me as I need it for the next meeting.
p. to sort out the mess, but you don't seem to be having much

success.

q. to switch off your computer before you leave the office.

r. to take out holiday insurance in case you should have to cancel for any reason.

s. to tell you but I'm afraid I never got round to it.

t. working twenty four hours a day like this, you're going to make yourself ill.

23

How to Do Well at Interviews
(Words Confused and Words Misused)

Choose the most appropriate answer from each pair of alternatives. But be careful because sometimes both answers might be correct!

So you have 1 <u>managed / succeeded</u> to secure a job interview for 2 <u>a position / a work</u> that 3 <u>fits / suits</u> you perfectly. Now comes 4 <u>a / the</u> moment of truth: How do you sell yourself and show your potential employer how valuable 5 <u>can you / you can</u> be to their company?

First, find out everything you can about the company you would be working for 6 <u>should / would</u> you get the job. Who are its customers? What is its mission statement? How does the job you would be performing relate to the company's goals? This will not only help you 7 <u>to work / work</u> out what questions to ask your interviewer 8 <u>and / but</u> it will also show them that you have 9 <u>done / made</u> your research.

Read over the job description carefully. Analyze your own strengths and see how you can tie the two together. If you have previous 10 <u>experience / experiences</u>, make a note of those times where you helped 11 <u>achieve / to achieve</u> a specific result. Employers 12 <u>give / pay</u> more serious consideration to applicants who have a background and a 13 <u>track / work</u> record in their industry 14 <u>than / then</u> those 15 <u>that / who</u> do not.

If your mind goes 16 <u>empty / blank</u> when asked if you have any questions, consider 17 <u>asking / to ask</u> why this particular position in the company has come up. Remember, you are not just selling yourself, but also trying to find out whether taking 18 <u>on / up</u> the job would actually be 19 <u>a / the</u> right move for you at this stage of your career.

And if you keep all of these suggestions 20 <u>in mind / on your mind</u>, you will not only have seriously impressed your potential employer, but you will come away from it feeling like a winner too! Good luck!

24

Built-in Obsolescence
(Words Confused and Words Misused)

Planned obsolescence or built-in obsolescence is the process of a product becoming obsolete or non-functional after a certain period or amount of use in a way that is planned or designed by the manufacturer. Planned obsolescence has potential benefits for a producer because the product fails and the consumer is under pressure to purchase again. The purpose of planned obsolescence is to hide the real cost per use from the consumer, and charge a higher price than they would otherwise be willing to pay (or would be unwilling to spend all at once).

Choose the most appropriate answer from each pair of alternatives. But be careful because sometimes both answers might be correct!

What really 1. gets on my nerves / makes me nervous is 2. a / the way nothing is 3. designed / made to 4. endure / last these days, and I am thinking in particular of 5. computers / the computers. To make matters 6. the worst / worse, 7. if / when you do decide to throw caution to 8. the wind / wind and spend all your hard-earned 9. cash / savings on a new laptop, one that is advertised as being the 10. last / latest model, you then 11. discover / find out a month later it has been discontinued and superseded by one which has even more impressive features. 12 A / The fact of 13 a / the matter is we are 14. continually / continuously being taken advantage 15. of / over in this way and I am completely sick and tired 16. of / with this. I would make a stand 17. against / for this if I could. 18. <u>However / Moreover,</u> 19. <u>being / to be</u> a writer I am totally dependent on 20. <u>having / to have</u> a decent computer so unfortunately I have no 21. <u>choice / say</u> in the matter.

25

Ethical Consumerism
(Words Confused and Words Misused)

Ethical consumerism is the intentional purchase of products and services that the customer considers to be made ethically. This may mean with minimal harm to or exploitation of humans, animals and/or the natural environment. Ethical consumerism is practiced through 'positive buying' in that ethical products are favoured, or 'moral boycott', that is negative purchasing and company-based purchasing.

Choose the most appropriate answer from each pair of alternatives. But be careful because sometimes both answers might be correct!

1 <u>Money / The money</u> makes the world 2 <u>go / to go</u> round, and deciding how 3 <u>do we spend / we spend</u> our money might just help us 4 <u>save / to save</u> it. To the ethical consumer, their money is a vote 5 <u>that / which</u> they use every time they go shopping. Food and goods in the UK are relatively cheap at the moment. But while we might be saving money, there's always 6 <u>a cost / a price</u> somewhere 7 <u>down / on</u> the line.

Buying cheap 8 <u>clothes / cloths</u> 9 <u>that / which</u> have been made in sweatshops is a vote for worker exploitation. Buying a 10 <u>gas / petrol</u> guzzling 4X4, especially if you are a city dweller, is a vote for climate change.

Factory farmed animals, 11 <u>meantime / meanwhile</u>, may make cheap meat but it comes at a price, on the quality of 12 life / living of the animal.

Even small, everyday purchases, such as coffee, tea, breakfast cereal, bread or bin-bags are a vote for something. Favouring organic 13 produce / products is a vote for environmental sustainability and fair trade is a vote for 14 human rights / the human rights. Considering ethical issues when we go shopping means taking impacts like this 15 into / on account.

As 16 buyers / consumers, we have a great deal of power in our pockets. 17 However / Moreover, sometimes the choices aren't straightforward. Is it better to buy organic vegetables flown in from overseas, or non-organic vegetables from a local farmer? Not everyone will come to 18 a / the same conclusion.

Ethical consumerism is just as much about supporting the 'good' companies and products as it is withdrawing our support from the 'bad' ones. This means 19 favouring / to favour particular ethical products, such as energy saving light bulbs and not buying products that you disapprove of, such as battery eggs. More often than not, the most effective way to do this is to target a business 20 as a whole / on the whole and to avoid all the products made by one company.

26

The Causes of Inflation
(Words Confused and Words Misused)

Choose the most appropriate answer from each pair of alternatives. But be careful because sometimes both answers might be correct.

One of the 1 <u>underlying / undermining</u> causes of 2 <u>inflation / the inflation</u> is the 3 <u>level / rate</u> of monetary demand in the economy - how much money is being spent. We can demonstrate this by 4 <u>considering / looking at</u> what happens when the prices of some products are rising. If consumers want to buy the same amount of all goods and services 5 <u>as / than</u> before, they will now have to spend more. 6 <u>However / Moreover,</u> this will only be possible if their incomes are rising, or 7 <u>alternately / alternatively</u> if consumers are 8 <u>prepared / willing</u> to spend a bigger 9 <u>portion / proportion</u> of their incomes and save less. But if total spending does not rise, then higher prices will mean consumers will have to buy less of what they want. Any fall in demand for goods and services will put downward pressure on prices. So although higher costs might result in some prices 10 <u>rising / to rise,</u> there cannot be a 11 <u>continued / sustained</u> rise in prices 12 <u>unless / until</u> incomes and spending are also rising.

On 13 <u>another / the other</u> hand, if the price of some goods 14 <u>falls / reduces,</u> people will need to spend less to buy the same amount 15 <u>as / than</u> before. But if people still earn the same, they will now be able to buy more of those goods or of something else. Demand in the economy will rise and this, in turn, might 16 cause / make some prices to rise.

But inflation is not just about demand in isolation. Inflation 17 is an indication of / reflects the amount of demand in the economy 18 related / relative to the available supply. For this reason, inflation 19 inclines / tends to rise when, at the current price level, demand is greater than the economy's output.

Firms can usually 20 heighten / increase production to meet higher demand, but often only by incurring higher costs. For example, it might be necessary to introduce 21 extra time / overtime working or 22 hire / rent extra people. If many firms are trying to 23 register / recruit extra people in order to produce more, wages might start to rise. And firms might have to pay more for additional materials, often imported from abroad. Imports are then likely to rise and the 24 trade balance / trade difference might widen as a result.

To contain inflationary pressures in the economy, though, demand needs to grow roughly 25 in line with / in a line with output.

27

Green Banking or Ethical Banking - What's the Difference?

Choose the most appropriate answer from each pair of alternatives. But be careful because sometimes both answers might be correct!

When it comes to 1 <u>choose / choosing</u> an eco-friendly option for your savings, it really is 2 <u>a / the</u> matter of personal 3 <u>preference / taste</u>. While green banking, 4 <u>that / which</u> deals with such matters as branch energy costs and "green" initiatives, will show that you are 5 <u>conscientious / conscious</u> about "doing your bit" today, ethical banking will show that you are more 6 <u>concerned / worried</u> about the long term 7 <u>affect / effect</u> of what your finances are used for by your bank. If you want to be really eco-friendly, there's nothing to 8 <u>prevent /stop</u> you 9 <u>from saving / to save</u> your money with both.

10 <u>Banks / The banks</u> and building societies make profit by lending 11 <u>money / the money</u> you invest to third parties at a higher rate of interest. This is 12 <u>common / the common</u> knowledge. What often isn't known is which companies the banks are lending your money to. For example, your money could be loaned to companies involved 13 <u>in / with</u> the fur trade, arms dealers, or multi-national companies with poor environmental records.

Functioning on 14 <u>a / the</u> 15 <u>principal / principle</u> that funds are only invested into businesses that can prove that they won't 16 <u>harm / injure</u> the environment, people around the world, or animals and 17 <u>the wildlife / wildlife,</u> 18 <u>an / the</u> idea behind ethical banking is that 19 <u>money / the money</u> you deposit is only invested in pro-eco firms.

Aside from 20 <u>a / the</u> fact that you'll feel better knowing you're supporting an eco-friendly project, sometimes environmentally-friendly banking can be wallet-friendly as well. 21 <u>However / Moreover,</u> it has to be 22 <u>said / told</u> that 23 <u>neither / none</u> of the providers offer any real financial incentives to join them. So what you ultimately decide to do with you hard-earned cash is really all 24 <u>about / down to</u> your social 25 <u>awareness / conscience</u>.

28

Noun Phrases with
Dependent Prepositions (i)

Complete the noun phrases with their dependent propositions, and then use them in the sentences. Use each noun phrase once only:

1.	be in contact	a.	about
2.	find a way	b.	at
3.	have access	c.	for
4.	have an advantage	d.	from
5.	have designs	e.	in
6.	have doubts	f.	of
7.	have a flair	g.	on
8.	have second thoughts	h.	over
9.	take comfort	i.	to
10.	take interest	j.	with

1. You need _____ no _____ my ability to do the job as it's something I've done many times before.

2. We somehow need to _____ reducing costs and cutting back on the number of staff we employ might be our only option.

3. You clearly _____ languages, which is why I think you'd be ideally suited to the job.

4. I have not been _____ anyone from head office for some time now so I am not really sure what is going on.

5. You clearly _____ information that I do not have, and in that respect you _____ me.

6. It's a great shame you _____ so little _____ the company as I was hoping that once I decide to retire you would take it over one day.

7. Instead of moaning and groaning all the time, you should _____ the fact that unlike the majority of us you even have a job.

8. I can assure you I _____no _____ your job whatever you might have heard.

9. I wish you would stop _____ me all the time because I'm doing the best that I can, and it's all that any man can do.

10. It's too late now to be _____ what you have done and you just have to learn how to live with it.

29

Noun Phrases with Dependent Prepositions (ii)

Complete the noun phrases with their dependent propositions, and then use them in the sentences. Use each noun phrase once only:

1.	be in two minds	a.	about
2.	gain control	b.	at
3.	gain an insight	c.	for
4.	give support	d.	from
5.	have confidence	e.	in
6.	have an effect	f.	into
7.	have knowledge	g.	of
8.	make allowances	h.	on
9.	take courage	i.	over
10.	take a look	j.	to

1. If you hope to _____ the company you will need to buy up a majority of the shares.

2. I _____ no _____ what was said at the meeting so it would be unfair of me to make any comments at this stage.

3. We have no reason to doubt your ability to do the job and we _____ every _____ you

4. You need to _____ the fact that he is new to the job and has never done this kind of work before.

5. We need to _____ our full _____ the changes that have been introduced, as they could well help to get us out of the mess we now find ourselves in.

6. You can _____ the fact that many others have had to face such a problem and have survived it, and you can do the same too.

7. She is _____ whether to accept the job or not. One of the problems is that it would involve relocating, and this could _____ a damaging _____ her relationship with her partner.

8. We need to _____ long hard _____ the effect such a move could have before we come to any final decision.

9. Neuro-Linguistic Programming is a useful tool that can help you _____ what makes other people tick.

30

Noun Phrases with
Dependent Prepositions (iii)

Complete the noun phrases with their dependent propositions, and then use them in the sentences. Use each noun phrase once only:

1.	be an expert	a. about
2.	be in the mood	b. at
3.	be of benefit	c. for
4.	get a grip	d. from
5.	get pleasure	e. in
6.	have feelings	f. of
7.	have qualms	g. on
8.	have regrets	h. over
9.	take advantage	i. to
10.	take part	j. towards

1. I hope you _____ no _____ what has happened because you did the best that you could.

2. It is clear now that the merger of the two companies would _____ everyone concerned.

3. I hope that everyone will agree to _____ the talks whatever their political affiliations might be.

4. You really need to _____ this opportunity because a chance like this might never present itself again.

5. I can assure you I _____ having to give you a written warning, but I really have no choice in the matter.

6. You seem to _____ putting yourself down and you really need to believe in yourself more.

7. I _____ working seven days a week if that is what is required to get the job done, and I expect everyone who works for me to take the same attitude too.

8. We must not let any personal _____ we may _____ each other get in the way of our relationship at work.

9. I am not _____ any more of your games so just give me a straight answer this time please.

10. You really need to _____ the situation because if you don't there is now a real danger that it could spiral out of control

31

Adjectives with
Dependent Prepositions (i)

Match the adjectives with their dependent propositions, and then use them in the sentences. Use each adjective with its dependent preposition once only:

1.	bemused	a. about
2.	blamed	b. by
3.	committed	c. for
4.	concerned	d. from
5.	depressed	e. into
6.	exempt	f. of
7.	hopeful	g. on
8.	intent	h. over
9.	obsessed	i. to
10.	tempted	j. with

1. Why am I always the one who gets _____ everything in this company when things go wrong?

2. We are _____ being able to resume services within the next 24 hours and will of course keep you informed.

3. You seem to be _____ cutting costs but I am not convinced that is really the solution to the problem.

4. Let me assure you that I am totally _____ turning the fortunes of this company around and will not rest until I have done so.

5. Not having an income makes you _____ paying income tax, but there is still paperwork involved.

6. It is only natural that you should be _____ the future of the company, but worrying about it is not going to help in any way.

7. Is there any way you could be _____ coming out of retirement or is your decision final?

8. I am rather _____ the role I am expected to be playing in the company and I would like a meeting to clarify the situation.

9. You must be _____ the way things have turned out, but all is not lost yet so don't give up hope.

10. Some people are so _____ reaching the top that they are not prepared to let anything stand in their way

32

Adjectives with
Dependent Prepositions (ii)

Match the adjectives with their dependent propositions, and then use them in the sentences. Use each adjective with its dependent preposition once only:

1.	annoyed	a.	about
2.	come close	b.	at
3.	confused	c.	by
4.	content	d.	for
5.	derived	e.	from
6.	good	f.	into
7.	inspired	g.	of
8.	proud	h.	over
9.	renowned	i.	to
10.	transformed	j.	with

1. You get _____ things too easily and you really need to learn how to be more patient.

2. The hotel is _____ the five-star service it provides and the new management is determined to ensure that this continues to be the case.

3. I have _____ handing in my notice on several occasions and the only thing that has stopped me from doing so is the fact that I now have a wife and a child to support.

4. Under your leadership the company has been _____ something truly extraordinary and you can be very _____ what you have achieved.

5. It is clear that you are not the sort of person who could be _____ being second-best and I just wish everybody shared your attitude.

6. I'm a bit _____ what I'm supposed to do so you'll have to explain it to me once again I'm afraid.

7. _____ your example, I have decided to hand in my notice and to go freelance too.

8. There are clear benefits to be _____ the strategic location of a business, which is precisely why we cannot consider taking on a place like this.

9. You're _____ what you do and so am I, which is why we should be able to work well together.

33

Uncountable Nouns (i)

Match the numbers on the left with the letters on the right, and then use the phrases in the sentences. Use each phrase once only.

1.	bonds of	a.	calling
2.	call for	b.	communication
3.	campaign of	c.	concern
4.	cause for	d.	confidence
5.	lack of	e.	discontent
6.	form of	f.	information
7.	medium for	g.	peace
8.	sense of	h.	satisfaction
9.	show of	i.	slavery
10.	sign of	j.	support
11.	source of	k.	trust
12.	time of	l.	uncertainty
13.	wealth of	m.	violence

1.   A _____ is not a quality you would expect to find in a leader. Consequently, when it manifests itself, it is clearly a _____.

2.   Debt has been described as the modern-day _____, because the borrower is slave to the lender.

3.   Government ministers gave a _____ for the belea-guered Prime Minister when he came under attack from the opposition in the House of Commons yesterday.

4. The _____ has unfortunately so far been largely ignored by the various parties involved in the conflict.

5. It is a _____ to be given some credit for our achievements, and a good leader will recognize this.

6. In a _____ global economic _____, comparisons to the Great Depression not surprisingly abound.

7. A _____ and intimidation by the authorities to resolve the conflict will ultimately achieve nothing.

8. Pioneering leaders tend to get drawn into their work because of a strong _____, rather than through a methodical, strategic decision-making process.

9. Programming languages are not only useful to command computers. Increasingly they are also a _____ human _____.

10. Your outburst at the meeting can only be interpreted as a _____ your _____ and for that reason perhaps it would be in your best interests to look for alternative employment.

11. Despite the fact that there is a _____ available on the website, I was unable to find what I was looking for, and will have to search elsewhere for what I need.

12. Close friends and family who share deep _____, love, and respect, are essential to enable us to find the courage to follow our chosen paths in life.

34

Uncountable Nouns (ii)

Match the numbers on the left with the letters on the right, and then use the phrases in the sentences. Use each phrase once only.

1. array	a. appreciation
2. case	b. barter
3. cause	c. contents
4. form	d. development
5. lack	e. discrimination
6. period	f. hardship
7. programme	g. information
8. realm	h. revenue
9. sense	i. stress
10. source	j. uncertainty
11. table	k. unease

1. During a _____ economic _____, the support of your family can make all the difference as to whether you manage to keep the wolf from the door or not.

2. Out-of-pocket payments were, and still are in most developing countries, the principal _____ for health services.

3. You should be able to find the Chapter you are looking for listed in the _____.

4. As part of your _____ continuous professional _____, you might like to consider taking one of these courses.

5. A _____ is growing in the country. If the mood cannot be precisely defined or wholly explained, it can be clearly felt.

6. With the advent of agriculture came the use of grain and other vegetable or plant products as a standard _____ in many cultures.

7. _____ is one of, if not the leading cause of job dissatisfaction, and it is important for those in managerial positions to be aware of this if they hope to hold on to valued members of staff.

8. A whole _____ is available these days on the Internet, but not all of it can be trusted. That is why great care needs to be taken, especially when buying goods or services online.

9. What you have described to me is clearly a _____ racial _____. No one is allowed to treat you that way, and you should get a lawyer and sue, not just for the injustice you have suffered, but for future employees who might have to put up with the same treatment you have been subjected to.

10. If you can figure out the underlying _____ of your job _____, then it is more than likely you will also be able to find a cure for it.

11. Many problems exist in the _____ that science cannot solve, and scientists are only deluding themselves if they think otherwise.

35

What Sort of Manager Are You?

Respond to each of the statements below by asking yourself if you do the action most of the time, sometimes or never.

1. Tell my staff honestly how they are doing.
2. I give both positive feedback and constructive criticism.
3. I openly communicate expectations.
4. I keep my employees informed about changes taking place within the company.
5. I ask for opinions and involve employees in decisions that affect them.
6. I do not use threats or intimidation.
7. I acknowledge extraordinary effort with praise and special recognition.
8. I take the time to explain new procedures thoroughly.
9. I make sure that my employees understand the training I provide.
10. I make sure my employees have the training and resources necessary to do their jobs.
11. I treat my staff with respect.
12. I am not afraid to admit when I am wrong or to apologize when required.

Now add up your points and check your score. Give yourself 3 points for the answer *Most of the Time,* 2 points for *Sometimes,* and 1 point for *Never.*

If you have 31 to 36 points: Congratulations! You appear to have some very strong managerial skills. You communicate openly with your staff by sharing information and helping them feel secure in their roles. You recognize the importance of setting expectations, you avoid negative reinforcement, and you graciously acknowledge a job well done. Your respect for your team is evident, and it's very likely that they feel the same way about you.

If you have 25 to 30 points: Your managerial skills are on the way to being great, though you may be struggling a bit with communication. Remember that communication is a two way street - share your expectations, your appreciation and your knowledge. But don't be afraid to ask your staff to share their thoughts as well. You know the right things to do. Now you just have to commit to doing them all the time. As a manager, consistency is incredibly important.

If you have 19 to 24 points: It looks like you still have a little work to do. Treating your subordinates with little respect, using intimidation to get your way, or failing to provide positive feedback - *even sometimes* - can have a tremendous impact on employee morale. The good news is this: you can definitely make some simple changes that will have a big impact. Use the list above to help you focus on the areas you need help with. There are plenty of books, seminars and workshops out there aimed at helping you become the leader you know you can be.

If you have 12 to 18 points: Not everyone is meant for management, and you need to face the facts: you responded with "never" to the majority of the statements above. Look at these items. A strong leader should be doing each of these things "most of the time". Sure, it's not always easy. But being a leader is tough. You have to be willing to listen to others, acknowledge your own mistakes, and communicate in a respectful manner. Take a good long look at the list above and ask yourself if you can meet these standards. And if you can't (or aren't willing to) maybe it's time to reconsider what role you are best suited to.

36

Who Are the People
Who Make a Difference to Our Lives?

1. Name the six wealthiest people in your country according to this year's Rich List.
2. Name the last six winners of the 100 metres athletics race in the Olympics.
3. Name six people who have won the Nobel Prize.
4. Name the last half dozen Academy Award winners for best actor and actress.

How did you do? The point is that none of us remember the headliners of yesterday. These are no second-rate achievers. They are the best in their fields. But the applause doesn't last forever and achievements are forgotten.

Here's another short quiz. See how you do on this one:

1. Name six people who have helped you through a difficult time in your life.
2. Name six people who have taught you something worthwhile.
3. Think of six people who have made you feel appreciated and special.
4. Think of six people you enjoy spending time with.

Easier? The lesson: The people who make a difference in your life are not the ones with the most credentials, the most money, or the most awards. They are the ones that care. So make sure in the place where you work that you are one of these people!

37

Conditionals (i)

Match the numbers with the letter to complete the sentences. The first one has been done for you as an example:

1. **If you are declared bankrupt,**
2. If you do not keep up the repayments on the mortgage
3. If the economic recovery is to continue
4. Dwindling levels of investment in training must rise
5. If you have worked continuously for the same employer for two years or more and are made redundant,
6. And if you are given notice of redundancy,
7. If you will keep turning up late for work,
8. Anyway, not to worry too much about it, for if the worst came to the worst and you lost your job,
9. If the order had been dispatched when it was supposed to have been, .
10. Were you to get the job
11. Unless sales pick up and soon,
12. If it wasn't for the fact that I enjoy the work I do,

a. all the problems we have subsequently had could have been avoided.
b. it is important that future skills development needs are correctly identified
c. if UK employers are to remain competitive
d. it's not surprising you have been given a verbal warning by your boss.
e. it looks as if we're going to have to close down.
f. it would mean all your financial worries could be laid to

rest. And what a relief that would be for you!

g. I would have left this company ages ago because the money I get paid is an insult.

h. **then the court will use any relevant money and assets that you have to pay off some or all of the money you owe. (This will be done by the Official Receiver if you have no assets to speak of and by an Insolvency Practitioner if you do have assets).**

i. then you could always come and work for me.

j. you are entitled to some paid time off to look for a new job - provided that, by the time your period of notice ends, you have been with the employer for two years.

k. you are likely to be entitled to statutory redundancy pay.

l. your property may be repossessed

1 h_ 2 __ 3 __ 4 __ 5 __ 6 __ 7 __ 8 __ 9 __ 10 __ 11 __ 12 __

38

Conditionals (ii)

Match the numbers with the letter to complete the sentences. The first one has been done for you as an example:

1. **If I had unlimited funds,**
2. Should you have any problems with the product for any reason,
3. Had it not been for all the hard work you put in,
4. If you are declared bankrupt,
5. If you are a limited company, though,
6. It seems I have no choice in the matter, but I wonder what you would do
7. I am afraid it is out of the question at the moment, but if there were to be an economic recovery,
8. If you take my advice,
9. Had it not been for your support and encouragement,
10. When two companies merge
11. If you will keep criticising your line manager,
12. Had we not decided upon a fallback position before the start of the negotiations,

a. anything you have of value can be taken, your house, car, bank accounts, the only thing they cannot take is the tools of your trade, e.g. plumbing equipment.
b. if you were in my position.
c. I never would have stayed here as long as I have. But now I feel it is time I made a move
d. it is a really stressful time for everyone involved in the process, especially the employees.

e. **I would not hesitate to invest in the venture.**

f. please let us know immediately.

g. the good news is they can only take what is involved with the company, and they cannot touch your house, car or personal bank account

h. then it is hardly surprising you were overlooked when the opportunity for a promotion came up.

i. then we would certainly consider the idea.

j. we never would have met the deadline.

k. we would never have been able to finalise the deal.

l. you will tell them exactly what you think of their derisory offer because for sure you can do a lot better.

1 e 2 __ 3 __ 4 __ 5 __ 6 __ 7 __ 8 __ 9 __ 10 __ 11 __ 12 __

39

Being Self-employed and How to Punctuate It!

Decide which of these sentences need commas inserted into them, where they should be placed, and why:

a. If you're self-employed you don't work for anyone except for yourself.

b. You don't work for anyone except for yourself if you're self-employed.

c. I'm currently self-employed. I have worked for companies in the past though.

d. I'm a self-employed person who would never make the mistake of working for a company again.

e. I'm self-employed which means I'm my own boss.

f. I'm self-employed. However I have sometimes worked for a company in the past.

g. I'm self-employed. Moreover it's a position I choose to be in.

h. Being self-employed I'm only answerable to myself.

i. In my opinion being your own boss is the ideal situation to be in.

j. I don't work for a company because I've found that it does not suit me.

40

Connectors and Modifiers (i)

Match the numbers with the letter to complete the sentences. The first one has been done for you as an example:

1. **The decision that was made not to invest in the project came as a blow,**
2. It is hoped significant progress can be achieved at these talks
3. We assured the organisers we could find our own way to the Conference venue,
4. In spite of the gloomy economic outlook,
5. Regardless of the reason for climate change,
6. However much you dislike your job,
7. As long as you are prepared to meet me half way,
8. In comparison to our competitors in the field,
9. Not only have most brands of bottled water been shown to have no health benefits over tap water,
10. It is unfair that I should be required to come to work in the office every day
11. Notwithstanding the fact that you have managed to somewhat reduce your overdraft,
12. Contrary to expectations and despite negative publicity,

a. **albeit not unexpected given the current economic climate.**
b. but nevertheless they insisted on accompanying us.
c. even though I could work from home.
d. I would like to think we have something more to offer our clients.

e. nevertheless your account still remains overdrawn and we need to discuss this with you at your earliest convenience.

f. our latest product has proved to be remarkably successful.

g. reaching a deal should be no problem.

h. some have even been shown to be inferior in quality to the water we get from our taps.

i. there are still plenty of jobs available for those prepared to go out and look for them.

j. what is clear is that we have got to do something about it and to do so now, before it becomes too late.

k. with a view to improving industrial relations that have unfortunately become somewhat strained.

l. you should be thankful that at least you have one.

1 a_ 2 __ 3 __ 4 __ 5 __ 6 __ 7 __ 8 __ 9 __ 10 __ 11 __ 12 __

41

Connectors and Modifiers (ii)

Match the numbers with the letter to complete the sentences. The first one has been done for you as an example:

1. **Considering the current social and economic climate,**
2. As a result of the economic downturn,
3. Given the problems we have been experiencing recently,
4. With reference to our telephone conversation today,
5. Despite the doom and gloom of the "credit crunch" and talks of recession,
6. Further to our discussion this morning,
7. Regarding your application,
8. In view of the current economic situation,
9. However much you offer it will make no difference,
10. Although I know it's not what you were hoping for,
11. Under the circumstances,
12. It would clearly be best for both sides

a. all our plans for expansion have been put on hold.
b. for the business is not for sale.
c. I'm afraid it's the best that I can do.
d. I am pleased to be able to announce that our company continues to buck the trend and continues to grow.
e. I am writing to confirm that your order has been dispatched and should be with you by the end of the month.
f. I believe it's a very fair offer and I doubt if anyone will better it.
g. if we could reach some kind of compromise.

h. I think you should take whatever job you can get.

i. it is remarkable the company is still solvent.

j. please find attached (in a Word document) the email we would like you to send to your members on our behalf.

k. the Admissions team is here to help you with any questions you may have and to support you through the process.

l. **which political party do you think would do the best job, and why?**

1 ⌊ 2 __ 3 __ 4 __ 5 __ 6 __ 7 __ 8 __ 9 __ 10 __ 11 __ 12 __

42

Proverbs About Work

Match the numbers with the letter to complete the proverbs. The first one has been done for you as an example:

1. **All work and no play**
2. Money is the root of
3. If a job's worth doing, it's worth
4. A bad workman always
5. Hard work
6. Many hands
7. Jack of all trades,
8. A woman's work
9. Business before
10. If you want a thing done well,
11. A golden key
12. If you pay peanuts,

a. all evil.
b. blames his tools.
c. can open any door.
d. doing well.
e. do it yourself.
f. is never done.
g. make light work.
h. **makes Jack a dull boy.**
i. master of none.
j. never did anyone any harm.
k. pleasure.
l. you get monkeys.

1 <u>h</u> 2 __ 3 __ 4 __ 5 __ 6 __ 7 __ 8 __ 9 __ 10 __ 11 __ 12 __

43

How Trustworthy Are You?

Are you doing your share to build the trust and increase your colleagues' and business associates' confidence in you? Find out by doing this quiz:

1. When I say I am going to do something, I do it.
    Always
    Sometimes
    Never

2. If I will be late making a commitment or getting to work, I call.
    Always
    Sometimes
    Never

3. I keep my colleagues' confidences and do not share them with other people.
    Always
    Sometimes
    Never

4. I am careful not to discuss information about my colleagues with other people.
    Always
    Sometimes
    Never

5. My colleagues can count on me to listen to concerns without judgment or ridicule.
   Always
   Sometimes
   Never

6. When staff meetings are held, you make sure that your line manager is clearly the most important person in the room.
   Always
   Sometimes
   Never

7. When I am angry with a colleague, I am careful not to use information that he or she has confided in me win the argument.
   Always
   Sometimes
   Never

8. I refrain from name-calling or sarcasm when I am upset with a colleague.
   Always
   Sometimes
   Never

44

How Ethical Are You at Work?

1. You have just printed a 200-page document that used up all the paper in the printer.
a. You refill the paper tray immediately.
b. You casually mention that the machine is out of paper to people around you so they know to refill it before they hit print.
c. You reckon they'll figure it out eventually in any case, so you do nothing.

2. Your boss hands you a stack of papers that accidentally includes confidential personnel files. You
a. Immediately return the files to your boss once you recognize the mistake.
b. Search through the pages just to find your own file.
c. Read everyone's files.

3. You're running late because you got a little too happy at last night's "happy hour" and overslept this morning.
a. You call ahead to warn your team you'll be late so they're not further inconvenienced by your non-appearance.
b. You show up late and hope no one notices.
c. You show up late and blame it on a horrible (imaginary) car crash that caused traffic to back up for miles.

4. You haven't had a day off in months and feel you'd like to take tomorrow off.
a. Tell your boss you could do with a break and would like to use up a day of your holiday allowance for the purpose.

b. Start coughing and mention you feel bad so that you've built a convincing reason to call in sick.

c. Wait until the morning when you know your boss hasn't arrived. Leave a message saying an emergency's come up and you can't make it in today.

5. In the middle of a boring business meeting, you realize you could be more productive (or less bored) if you were at your desk instead. You

a. Grin and bear it because it would be rude to leave.

b. Pretend to have received an urgent call or e-mail and go back to your desk to work.

c. Pretend you need to go to the toilet, but go back to your desk and update your Facebook instead.

6. You find out a colleague you share your office with is having a secret affair with someone in accounting.

a. You pretend you know nothing about it.

b. You tell your closest work friends because you know they won't tell anyone.

c. You tell anyone who will listen

7. You have just accepted a job offer at a new company. It begins in a month, so you're going to wait two weeks to give your notice. The next day your boss comes in and explains how he wants to restructure the department and your role is pivotal.

a. To prevent his plans from going awry, you decide to tell him now that you're leaving in a month.

b. You go along with his plans for now, but still give your two weeks' notice so that he receives ample warning time and you aren't let go a month before your new job starts.

c. You wait until your last day to tell him that you're leaving and that it was nice knowing him.

8. You know the boss is in a terrible mood. You also know your co-worker is about to go ask the boss for a ridiculously large pay rise.
a. You quietly warn your colleague that the boss is probably going to throw scissors at him if he goes in there today.
b. You mind your own business because you don't want to get involved.
c. You don't mention the boss' bad mood and instead get your colleague fired up and encourage him to triple the salary request.

9. It is 3 p.m. on Christmas Eve and the office is empty because everyone else is away on holiday already. The phone hasn't rung once and no e-mails have come in.
a. You stay at your desk until 5 p.m. because it's your job.
b. You wait 30 more minutes to make sure nothing comes up, and then you leave.
c. Ha! You've been gone since noon.

10. Your boss loves the ideas you pitched to everyone and can't stop showering you with accolades. The problem is that the ideas were actually a joint effort between you and your colleague.
a. You say, "Thanks, but I didn't work alone. Sheila worked just as hard as I did."
b. You take the praise, and eventually tell Sheila what happened and that you didn't know how to tell the boss.
c. You accept the accolades and try to get Sheila fired before she finds out you've stolen all the glory.

45

How Satisfied Are You with Your Job?

Do you love your job or are you one of the many unfortunate people who spend their time at work daydreaming about being somewhere (or anywhere) else? Take this quiz to help you find out if you are in the right job or not. Read each statement and give yourself one point for each one you agree with:

1. You make positive comments about your job when people ask what you do or how work is going.
2. You have a developed a positive relationship with your colleagues, or at least learned how to deal with each other's different personalities.
3. You feel included in decision-making and truly believe that your opinion matters at work.
4. The people you work with treat you as an equal, even though you may have less experience than they do.
5. You have managed to find a healthy balance between your work and personal life and both benefit as a result.
6. You find people look to you for advice at work.
7. You're ready for and even excited about the upcoming projects you'll be working on.
8. Your line manager is supportive and offers you good advice and opportunities for further professional development.
9. You feel positive about what the company is doing, and feel that you really make a difference or contribution.
10. Even though like most of us you could use some more money, your salary is basically a fair one.
11. You feel like you are in the right field for your interests,

skills and personality.

12. There may be some repetitive or boring parts about your job, but for the most part you are stimulated.

13. Stressful situations may arise, but you don't feel too overwhelmed or stressed-out on a regular basis.

14. You feel healthy at work and don't regularly worry or feel sick about going in the next day.

15. Fear of debt or not being able to find another job aren't the sole reasons you're sticking around. You actually quite enjoy what you do.

Scores:

0-3: You have little to no satisfaction with your work. You may feel undervalued, or a job that was once challenging has now come to a standstill. Consider whether it's the job itself or the company that is making you unhappy and find a place or career that changes that.

4-6: You have some satisfaction with your job, whether it's the relationship you've developed with the people you work with or the work itself that you're doing. However, you may want to consider where this career is taking you and a change of direction might be what is required at this point in time.

7-9: Overall, you're satisfied with your job, but you may feel a little overwhelmed or stressed at times, and probably wish that you had more time to balance your work and personal life.

10-12: You are really satisfied with your job and while you look around once in a while to see what else is available, it's only because you want to consider your options, know your value, and keep your mind on where your career is heading.

13-15: Congratulations! You have a job that you find challenging in a company where you feel valued so make sure you hold on to it. Money isn't the sole driver of getting you out of bed in the morning, passion is, which is just how it should be.

46

Plural Nouns / Uncountable Nouns

Fill the gaps in the following sentences with either an uncountable or a plural noun. Use each noun once only:

accommodation / advice / baggage / conditions / consideration / earnings / guesswork / harm / insurance / jeans / outgoings / progress / room / rubbish / savings / takings / tidings / timing / trainers / valuables

1. You are one of several candidates under _____ but we have come to no decision as yet.
2. I have been thinking about investing in property but I am not really sure what to do with my _____. What would your _____ be?
3. We have a strict dress code in this company, which means no _____ or _____.
4. You need to cut out all the _____ and to focus on the facts in your report.
5. We are pleased to announce that the "buy one, get one free" promotion in the store has led to an increase in _____ this month.
6. I've never heard such a load of _____ before, and it's clear you have no idea what you're talking about.
7. I would advise you to deposit all your _____ in the hotel safe.
8. Although some _____ has been made in the talks, we still have a long way to go.
9. The tax you will be required to pay is dependent on how high your _____ are.

10. To make sure you come to no _____, we recommend you go nowhere on your own and that you stay with the group at all times.

11. I wish I had some good _____ to bring you, but it is all doom and gloom these days I'm afraid.

12. The working _____ here are disgraceful and it is beyond me how you mange to put up with them.

13. To assess the potential profitability of the company, we would need to know what your monthly _____ are.

14. Although we will pay for both your air fare and _____, you will have to cover the cost of travel _____ and for any excess _____ you may have.

15. _____ is crucial to ensure the successful launch of the product, and there is no _____ for any mistakes.

47

Gerund or Infinitive

Shakespeare's most famous words are probably "To be or not to be", but perhaps they should have been "To be or being" because that is the really difficult question in English. Some verbs are always followed by the gerund - the ING form of the verb, whereas others are always followed by the infinitive with TO. Match the halves of the following sentences together, and then arrange the verbs used in the sentences into two columns in the Table:

1. I cannot possibly **imagine** what it would be like
2. Although I **considered**
3. I **attempted**
4. Despite having reservations about your performance to date, we have **decided**
5. The main reason why I **enjoy**
6. You need to be patient for a short while longer because we **hope**
7. Fortunately we **managed**
8. Although I **offered**
9. You really must **resolve**
10. If we can't reach a compromise, it looks as if we'll just have to **agree**
11. What I really want to know is how you are **planning**
12. I don't **mind**
13. If you act too hastily, you could **risk**
14. The problem is you **keep**
15. I fully understand the way you feel as I would **resent**

a. being my own boss is that nobody can tell me what I have to do any more.

b. handing in my notice, I came to the conclusion that it was not in my best interest to do so.

c. having to work for someone I had no respect for too.

d. losing everything so take your time over this.

e. making mistakes and it is costing the company a great deal of money that we simply do not have.

f. not having to work for a living.

g. to disagree.

h. to do better in future or else your job could be at risk.

i. to get us out of this mess.

j. to give you one more chance to show us what you can do.

k. to have better news to report very soon.

l. to help them to complete the job, they said I was surplus to requirements.

m. to persuade them to change their minds but at the end of the day there was nothing more I could do.

n. to set aside our differences and our intention is to work together in future.

o. working overtime in order to meet the deadline just as long as I get paid for it.

Verbs always followed by DOING	Verbs always followed by TO DO

48

Everything You Always Wanted
to Know About Asking for a Pay Rise

Place the following stages in the process of asking for a pay rise in the correct order:

a. After all, if your current boss turns down your request, your position in the company would be much weaker if you still stayed.

b. And if the worst should come to the worst and they refuse to meet your demands, try and arrange a time when your position can be reviewed again. Remember that many bosses are unlikely to give you any extra reward simply for doing your job well - that's what you're paid to do.

c. Firstly, make a list of your current responsibilities, achievements, workload, and all the positive aspects you have brought to the job.

d. Getting a new job offer, though, can be risky. To use an offer as a bargaining tool you must be prepared to leave, so if you are not completely certain that you want the new job but are just attracted by the money you should forget it.

e. If, for instance, you want a £2,000 pay rise then it may be an idea to ask for £4,000 in the knowledge your boss may meet you around half way.

f. Pay rises are notoriously difficult to achieve. There are, however, two obvious main ways of getting more cash.

g. Request a private word. When you are called in, thank your boss for his time and then get straight to the point.

h. Requesting a pay rise on the back of performance requires planning and a deft touch.

i. Say how much you enjoy the job and briefly run through your achievements. Then let him or her know what you are after.

j. Success will come down to the way you approach your boss and the amount of money that is available. It is important to be clear about what you want and also to have evidence to back up your claims

k. The first is by getting another job offer and the second is by demonstrating you are doing far more than your contract stipulates.

l. Then decide how much extra money you want - or if you would accept improved terms such as a better car, grander title or shares in the company. Be prepared to haggle.

1 ___ 2 ___ 3 ___ 4 ___ 5 ___ 6 ___ 7 ___ 8 ___ 9 ___ 10 ___ 11 ___ 12 ___

49

Everything You Always Wanted to Know About Going Bankrupt

The word bankruptcy is derived from two old English words, "bankus" which means a tradesman's table and "ruptus" which means to break. In former times, only traders could be made bankrupt and they were then subjected to punishments such as the stocks and "the clink" - the debtors' prison where day release was granted to allow debtors to work so they could pay off their debts. These days anyone who owes more than £750 can technically be made bankrupt. However, you cannot be made bankrupt overnight and it is only if you have received a statutory demand or have a judgement made against you that a creditor can begin bankruptcy proceedings.

Now place the following stages of the process in the correct order:

a. A final word of warning, for anyone considering the transfer of assets or giving money to family or friends in the run-up to bankruptcy, it is not advisable.

b. After the end of the 12-month period, provided you have co-operated fully, then your bankruptcy is discharged and all your debts are written off.

c. After this minimum period of time, there will then be a hearing and you will need to attend court. The hearings are normally short and the date and time that you are made bankrupt is noted.

d. At the start of bankruptcy proceedings, you will normally be personally served with a bankruptcy petition. From the time that petition is filed at court, you then have at least 28 days to pay the debt or have it removed.

e. Bankruptcy generally lasts for one year, during which you cannot act as a director of a limited company or be involved in the management of a company.

f. Either way, before the Official Receiver makes that decision, he will interview you either in person or by telephone. All your creditors must now deal with the Official Receiver and cannot continue to contact you directly.

g. They review your affairs and decide whether your case is sufficiently complicated to be passed on and handled by a private insolvency practitioner or if it will remain with the Official Receiver.

h. This is because any transfer you make within five years of your bankruptcy can be reversed, unless it is a sale for proper value.

i. You can incur credit, though, provided you inform the person giving you credit that you are bankrupt, and you can operate a bank account. And you can, and should, seek gainful employment during your bankruptcy.

j. Your financial affairs are then passed to the government department called the Official Receiver to be dealt with.

1 ___ 2 ___ 3 ___ 4 ___ 5 ___ 6 ___ 7 ___ 8 ___ 9 ___ 10 ___

50

One Word, Three Uses (i)

Find one word only which can be used appropriately in all three sentences. Here is an example:

You've been overworking recently and you really need to ... a break.

Perhaps the most sensible thing to do would be to ... some time out to reconsider your position before you come to any decisions regarding your future.

There's been a great improvement in the company's figures and it is the sales team who should ... most of the credit for it.

Answer: take.

Q1

A job like this would be right up your _____ so why don't you apply for it?

I agree with you one hundred per cent but I am not sure the man in the _____ would.

You're _____s ahead of all your main competitors and so you have nothing to worry about.

Answer: _____

Q2

The truth is that you _____ head and shoulders above all the other candidates for the job, and it will be nothing short of a crime if you don't get it.

The presentation you gave was truly out_____ing and you should be very proud of yourself.

Whatever happens there is one thing you can be sure of, which is that I promise I will _____ by you.

It's time we made a _____ against ageism in the workplace because there really is no place for it in our modern day and age.

Answer: _____

Q3

As is the case in any relationship, if there is to be any chance of an agreement, there needs to be _____ and take.

Although I'm not sure your plan is going to work, I am prepared to _____ it a go.

As we have absolutely no chance of winning the contract, we might as well _____ up and go home.

They say it's not over until the fat lady sings so it would be premature to _____ up the ghost just yet, especially with there being so much at stake.

Answer: _____

Q4

I was worried they would decide to take disciplinary action against me but fortunately I'm in the _____.

As soon as the weather _____s up a bit, I hope to start cycling to work each day once again.

Although both candidates have the same qualifications, when it comes to the issue of who has the most experience, there is a _____ difference between the two of them

Answer: _____

Q5

As we seem to do nothing but argue these days, I think the only solution is if we have a clean ____ from each other.

As it is such an important occasion, I have decided to _____ the habit of a lifetime and have a glass of champagne to celebrate the event.

It's true I could do with a new car, but I'm not prepared to
_____ the bank just so as I can have one.

As your office is so close to mine, perhaps we could meet up
during my lunch _____ tomorrow to catch up with things.

You've been working really hard and you deserve a ____ from
it all, which is why I have organised a weekend in Paris for
you.

Answer: _____

Q5

I have no idea whether things are going to work out all right.
It's all up in the _____ at the moment.

You have every right to _____ your views on the subject to me
in private, but not to anyone outside these four walls.

When I learnt we had been awarded the contract, I felt as if I
was floating on _____ .

What you had to say on the subject was like a breath of fresh
_____ , and the only original suggestion I heard all day.

Answer: _____

Q6

I never in a million years thought I would see you here – that's
a real _____-up for the books!

You scratch my back and I'll scratch yours. In other words, if
you do me a good _____ , then I'll see what I can do for you.

Unfortunately the patient seems to have taken a _____ for the
worse over the last 24 hours, and is back in intensive care
again.

I'm afraid you'll just have to wait as it's still not your _____
yet.

Answer: _____

51

One Word, Three Uses (ii)

Find one word only which can be used appropriately in all three sentences. Here is an example:

You've been overworking recently and you really need to
_____ a break.

Perhaps the most sensible thing to do would be to _____ some time out to reconsider your position before you come to any decisions regarding your future.

There's been a great improvement in the company's figures and it is the sales team who should _____ most of the credit for it.

Answer: take

Q1

It looks as if we have run out of _____ and it's time to place a new order.

In view of everything that has happened, we need to take _____ of the situation and perhaps have a rethink.

The company spokesperson gave all the usual _____ answers to the interviewer's questions so we learnt nothing new at all.

The area around London where rich people who work in the city live is known as _____broker belt.

Answer: _____

Q2

Tired of being unable to find a job in this country, I decided the best thing to do was to make a _____ break and emigrate.

Firms naturally prefer to start with a _____ sweep when setting up a new subsidiary.

It time you came _____ about what your real motives are and stopped trying to pull the wool over our eyes.

Answer: _____

Q3

Why don't you _____ your boss out and see what she has to say about it? You might find she's in favour of the idea too.

Although a recovery in sales has been reported, most retailers are still _____ ing a note of caution.

When I looked across the room to where my colleague was sitting, I noticed he was _____ asleep.

By the _____ of things, and despite all the rumours that have been flying around recently, it would seem that the company is actually doing reasonably well.

Answer: _____

Q4

It is perfectly normal to feel _____sick on occasions when you are obliged to work overseas for any length of time.

Now that we are finally on the _____ straight and the job is nearly finished, we can afford to relax a bit.

Aside from London, Barcelona is one of my favourite cities and it's like a _____ from _____ for me.

You made out a convincing case in favour of the proposed changes, and the points you made struck _____.

Answer: _____

Q5

I would like to _____ your attention to the dress code of the company, which makes it clear you are expected to wear a suit and tie to work.

Although it was a really close _____ , luckily we managed to catch the connecting flight in the end.

Unfortunately there is no longer much _____ for the product, and this has been reflected in the recent sales figures.

If you _____ in sick on our busiest day of the year, how do you expect me to react? I will resist the temptation to _____ your honesty into question, though, as it would be more than my job is worth.

As so little interest has been shown in holding the event, the safest thing to do is probably to _____ the whole thing off.

Answer: _____

Q6

None of the candidates really stood out, but I would say John seemed the _____ of the bunch. What do you think?

What I want to know is why you are always trying to _____ an argument with me, and what it is that I have done to upset you so much.

What you did was to create an awful mess and then I was left to _____ up the pieces.

You can't just _____ and choose which jobs you do in this office – that's not the way it works here.

Answer: _____

52

One Word, Three Uses (iii)

Find one word only which can be used appropriately in all three sentences. Here is an example:

You've been overworking recently and you really need to _____ a break.

Perhaps the most sensible thing to do would be to _____ some time out to reconsider your position before you come to any decisions regarding your future.

There's been a great improvement in the company's figures and it is the sales team who should _____ most of the credit for it.

Answer: take

Q1

There's no point in trying to hide anything because we will find out anyway, so it is better to be _____ about your past.

I know you don't share my views, but all I ask is that you keep an _____ mind until you've heard what I have to say.

We welcome with _____ arms any suggestions you may have for improving the service we offer to our clients.

I have some ideas about the direction we should take in future but, at the same time, I am also _____ to suggestions.

Now that the problem is out in the _____ , hopefully steps can be taken to resolve it.

Answer: _____

Q2

I know you're really upset about what's happened but you

need to hold yourself in _____ somehow.

Why do you keep _____ing up on me to see what I'm doing? If you have so many doubts, you shouldn't have employed me in the first place!

Somehow we need to cut costs, and to do that we need to keep spending in _____.

I'd be grateful if you could _____ through this document for me to make sure I haven't made any mistakes.

Answer: _____

Q3

I'm going to plan everything right down to the last detail because I don't want to _____ anything to chance.

You just do whatever you want without so much as a by your _____ and I'm completely fed up with this.

If you think there's any chance of your being given a rise, you must have taken _____ of your senses!

I'm determined to get to the bottom of the problem and, in order to get there, I'll _____ no stone unturned.

Answer: _____

Q4

I wouldn't take on the job if I were you because you could _____ yourself in for a great deal of trouble.

He'll be really gutted that he didn't get the job so you'll need to _____ him down gently.

She would like to _____ it be known that she no longer works for the company.

We all need an out_____ for our aggression and mine is kickboxing.

Answer: _____

Q5

It's no clear to me at all who is in _____ of this company, and that's where the problem lies.

By way of an apology for all the inconvenience you've had, we have decided to offer you an upgrade, and it's completely free of _____.

So I would like you all now to _____ your glasses and join me in a toast to the happy couple. To John and Mary!

If you could get away for a few days to re_____ your batteries, I'm sure you'd feel completely different about things.

Answer: _____

Q6

You would _____ well to listen to the advice they have to offer you because they know what they are talking about.

It wouldn't _____ for someone in your position to be seen dressed that way.

I wish you had more self belief and that you wouldn't _____ yourself down all the time.

If that's the way you're going to behave, then I don't want to have anything to _____ with you!

Answer: _____

53

S-Word Puzzle

Answer the numbered clues across, with six letter words that include the letter S, to complete the grid:

1	S					
2		S				
3			S			
4				S		
5					S	
6						S
7						S
8					S	
9				S		
10			S			
11		S				
12	S					

1. the money you earn each month
2. I can _____ you have nothing to worry about and that your money is safe with us.
3. I can't carry on working here under these conditions so you leave me with no choice but to _____
4. You still have an important _____ to learn, which is that money doesn't grow on trees.
5. I wonder if you could possibly do me a favour _____
6. As _____ in the shops keep rising but the money I earn remains the same, I'm finding it increasingly difficult to manage these days.
7. In times of economic _____nobody's job is safe, no matter

how well qualified or experienced you may be.

8. I'll do the job for you if you _____, but I'm not at all happy about it.

9. Where one door _____ another opens, so you really mustn't get so upset about what has taken place.

10. In American English your CV is known as a _____

11. I was advised to _____ my money in stocks and shares but I felt it would be too risky so I opted for a savings account instead

12. The pressure to meet the deadline that has been set is causing me a great deal of _____

54

F-Word Puzzle

Answer the numbered clues across, with six letter words that include the letter F, to complete the grid:

1	F					
2		F				
3			F			
4				F		
5					F	
6						F
7						F
8					F	
9				F		
10			F			
11		F				
12	F					

1. I wonder if you could do me a _____ please.
2. If you delay booking your holiday until just a few days beforehand, there might be some special last-minute _____ available.
3. If you're hoping to make a good impression, you really need to make more of an _____
4. What all companies hope to make!
5. It has become clear that not only are you _____ of ideas, but that you are also not up to the job.
6. It's a _____ to know that I'm not the only person to feel this way.
7. It is my firm _____ that such a short-sighted policy can

only lead to disaster.

8. The most effective way to _____ dissatisfied customers is not necessarily by offering them compensation, but simply by saying sorry.

9. If all you have is instant _____, then I'd rather have a cup of tea please.

10. What we're looking for is a team player, but you seem to _____ working on your own.

11. The last thing I wanted to do was to _____ you so please accept my apologies.

12. Millions of private-sector workers face a pay _____ or cuts because of the economic crisis, while employees in the public sector are enjoying pay rises.

55

UK Water Imports 'Unsustainable'
(Word Formation)

For each gap, use the given root word to make the correct form of the missing word:

The amount of water used to produce food and goods imported to developed countries is 1 _____ [worse] water 2 _____ [short] in the developing world. To give but one example, two-thirds of the water used to make UK imports is used outside its borders. This is clearly 3 _____ [sustain], though, given population growth and climate change. And if countries such as the UK fail to help poorer nations curb water use and take account of how their water 4 _____ [foot] is impacting on the rest of the world, the water crisis will become 5 _____ [critic].

As the world's population continues to grow, so does the 6 _____ [globe] demand for food and energy, and the need for fresh water rises 7 _____ [correspond] too. But the fact is that developing countries are already using significant proportions of their water to grow food and produce goods for 8 _____ [consume] in the West, and this burgeoning demand from developed countries is putting severe 9 _____ [press] on areas that are short of water even now.

Water used to grow food and make things is known as "embedded water". Embedded in a pint of beer, for example, is about 130 pints (74 litres) of water - the total amount needed to grow the ingredients and run all the processes that make the pint of beer. A cup of coffee embeds about 140 litres (246 pints) of water, a cotton T-shirt about 2,000 litres, and a kilogram of steak 15,000 litres.

Using this 10 _____ [method], UK consumers see only about 3% of the water 11 _____ [use] they are 12 _____ [response] for. The average UK consumer uses about 150 litres per day, the size of a large bath. Ten times as much is embedded in the British-made goods bought by the average UK consumer; but that represents only about one-third of the total water embedded in all the average consumer's food and goods, with the 13 _____ [remain] coming from imports.

The same pattern can be seen in most developed countries and it cannot be allowed to continue. Instead, as 14 _____ [consider] and 15 _____ [care] members of society, it is our duty to help curb water use in the developing world, where about one billion people already do not have sufficient access to clean drinking water.

In order for this to happen, UK-funded aid projects should have water 16 _____ [conserve] as a central tenet, while companies should 17 _____ [exam] their supply chains and reduce the water used in them. This could lead to difficult questions being asked, though, such as whether it is right for the UK to import beans and flowers from water-stressed countries such as Kenya. While growing crops such as these uses water, selling them brings foreign 18 _____ [change] into poor nations.

In the West, concerns over water could eventually lead to goods carrying a label denoting their embedded water content, in the same way as 19 _____ [electric] goods now sport information about their energy 20 _____ [consume].

56

R-Word Puzzle

Answer the numbered clues across, with six letter words that include the letter R, to complete the grid:

#						
1	R					
2		R				
3			R			
4				R		
5					R	
6						R
7						R
8					R	
9				R		
10			R			
11		R				
12	R					

1. I can _____ you saying something very similar the last time we discussed the subject together.

2. It can be _____ argued that both sides are partly to blame for the current impasse.

3. If you can't raise the necessary finance, you will have to find someone to _____ the money from.

4. I _____ to inform you that you have not been short-listed on this occasion, as we have been able to draw on a shortlist of candidates whose experience and skills more closely match the requirements of the vacancy.

5. Nobody can possibly know what the _____ will bring. All we can do is to make educated guesses.

6. I wouldn't even _____ to try if I were you. It's just not worth the effort.
7. It doesn't really _____ what you think because it's not going to change a thing.
8. When we _____ more than we export, the result is a balance of trade deficit.
9. What a broker buys and sells
10. Initially it was just an isolated problem, but unfortunately it seems to have _____
11. To obtain more _____ for the product, we need to find new markets.
12. I'd _____ not talk about it, if you don't mind.

57

L-Word Puzzle

Answer the numbered clues across, with six letter words that include the letter L, to complete the grid:

1	L						
2		L					
3			L				
4				L			
5					L		
6							L
7							L
8						L	
9					L		
10			L				
11		L					
12	L						

1. In a bitter conflict like the one we are currently experiencing, there are no winners – only _____

2. Having a video conference rather than meeting in person _____ us to save a lot of time

3. What you clearly need is more _____ in yourself because without it nothing is possible

4. As long as you _____ the instructions, nothing can go wrong.

5. There is nothing you can do to change the situation so any resistance on your part to the proposed changes would just be _____

6. The price customers are charged for a product is the

_____ price.

7. To make sure nothing can possibly go wrong, absolutely everything needs to be planned for – right down to the very last _____.

8. What I would like to know is when you are going to _____ your account with us as payment is long overdue.

9. The fact that the pound has _____ in value means that foreign holidays now cost more.

10. _____ you can somehow find a way to resolve your personal issues, then you are not going to get very far.

11. They say a bad workman always _____ his tools, and unfortunately it would seem to be true in your case.

12. Turning the company around took a lot _____ than we had expected to, but fortunately we got there in the end.

58

How to Give an Effective Presentation

Most people get anxious about giving presentations, and there would probably be something wrong with you if you did not. The twelve tips below are designed both to help you to overcome your fears and to ensure that your presentation works. However, five of the tips are definitely not to be followed if you would like everything to go according to plan. Now see if you can find them:

1. Know your subject. Read through your presentation beforehand. Read around the subject, so that you are confident that you know more than your audience, even after you have spoken. If you know your subject then you will come across in an interesting way and keep the attention of your audience.
2. Expect to do well. Your expectations are obvious in your body language. If your audience sees that you expect to do badly, you will do badly. Expectation is vital.
3. Avoid the temptation to look members of the audience in the eye as people find this intimidating. Instead, look down whenever possible.
4. Always read from notes so you make no mistakes that you might later have cause to regret. Accuracy should always be your primary concern.
5. Slow your speech down. This makes you appear more confident and enables your audience to take it in more easily. If you are talking slower, it is easier for your audience to maintain their attention, and momentary lapses in their concentration mean that they miss less.

6. Shout to make sure everyone in the room can hear you and that nobody misses any of the points you wish to make. The latest research proves beyond any shadow of a doubt that this is the most effective way to get your message across.

7. Don't stand motionless like a dummy. Use your hands and keep moving around as this will help to hold the attention of the audience.

8. Keep your hands and thumbs visible. Holding your hands out, with the thumbs uppermost is a very powerful dominance gesture. Watch politicians speaking, they all use this gesture.

9. Rejoice in the endorphin high that you will feel when it goes well. Enjoy that special moment because you have earned it!

10. If you should have a bad experience, it means you are probably not cut out for public speaking and in future it would be best to leave the job to someone else instead who does have the ability and confidence required.

11. Make sure you are properly prepared. One hour of preparation is recommended for every minute of the speech, which means a 15-minute speech might require two days of work. It is also advisable to keeping presentations to a maximum of 30 minutes. If you are forced to go longer, take a break so audience members can stretch and refocus.

12. Improvise. It is always preferable to give a spontaneous presentation rather than a meticulously planned one. This is because what you have to say will come across more naturally and you are more likely to create a good impression this way.

59

What a Person Does for a Living
(Defining Clauses)

Find twelve occupations by matching each word in group A with a word from group B. then fit the occupations into the definitions:

GROUP A: civil / customs / dental / faith / fitness / flight / general / interior / life / spin / traffic / tree

GROUP B: attendant / coach / decorator / healer / hygienist / instructor / officer / practitioner / servant / spin / traffic / tree

The definitions:

1. A _____ is someone who provides advice and support to people who want to improve their lives.
2. A _____ is someone who works for a government department.
3. A _____ is someone who deals with trees that are damaged or affected by disease, especially by cutting off the damaged parts.
4. A _____is someone who ask you if you have any goods to declare when you enter a country.
5. A _____ is someone who uses prayer to make people well.
6. A _____ is someone who gives journalists information that makes a politician or organisation look as good as possible.
7. A _____ is someone who teaches you how to exercise.

8. A _____ is someone who looks after passengers on a plane.
9. A _____ is someone who cleans people's teeth and gives them advice on how to care for them.
10. A _____ is a family doctor who works in general practice.
11. A _____ is someone who checks that vehicles are legally parked.
12. A _____ is someone who creates the way the inside of a room or building looks by choosing the colour of the walls, the floor covering, and the style of the furniture.

The definitions above all contain defining clauses – essential information without which the sentences are incomplete. Defining clauses used to refer to people are introduced with WHO or THAT.

Defining clauses used to refer to things are introduced with WHICH or THAT. For example: The exercise WHICH / THAT you have just completed was on defining clauses.

60

How to Produce the Perfect CV

Find the missing words in the following text:

The recruiter who receives your CV will probably have loads to sort through and very little time in which to do the job, so your CV will have to showcase your relevant experience, skills and qualities as succinctly as possible. Simplification is the 1 _____ to success

STRUCTURE YOUR CV.

The most important information should be clearly 2 _____ out at the very beginning of your CV, as it's this that will get you long-listed for an interview. Don't 3 _____ the recruiter will search through reams of information to find out if you're qualified for a position – they won't!

KEEP IT SHORT

Whilst there's no 4 _____ and fast rule for the length of a CV, a couple of pages are usually 5 _____ as the norm. Keep it punchy, get your 6 _____ in the door and 7 _____ the more involved explanations for your interview.

KEEP IT SWEET

Your CV should not become a confessional, a list of mishaps or a series of excuses. Exorcise any references to failure – 8 _____ that's examination, marital or business. Instead, write positively and 9 _____ your best face to the world.

MAKE IT LOOK GOOD

Decorative patterns and eccentric formatting can often 10 _____ from your message. Keep your CV uncluttered with short sentences, big margins around your text and key points emphasised. Bullet 11 _____ can be useful, but in moderation.

TAILOR YOUR CV

A 12 _____ -fire way to boost your chances of getting an interview is to tweak your CV for each application you make. So go through the job spec with a fine tooth 13 _____, making sure to include examples proving relevant experience for all requirements of the role.

DON'T LEAVE SUSPICIOUS GAPS

Any unexplained gap in your employment history will create suspicion, so make sure to 14 _____ those holes. Even times of unemployment can be adequately 15 _____ if you focus on the development of soft skills such as project management, communication or teamwork.

CHECK, CHECK, CHECK. AND THEN CHECK AGAIN

Any spelling or grammatical mistakes in your CV are going to create a negative 16 _____ in the 17 _____ of the recruiter – why would they want to employ someone slapdash? Spell-checkers can often 18 _____ up erroneously altering words to American spelling conventions so don't rely on them. Instead, ask people you can trust to go over your CV for typos and grammatical errors.

DITCH THE SNAPSHOT AND PERSONAL INFO.

Unless specifically asked to provide a photo of yourself, 19 _____ it out. The skills, achievements and experience you describe should 20 _____ weight with the recruiter, not your hairstyle or any other personal information unless strictly 21 _____ to your application.

BE HONEST

Never, ever 22 _____ the truth in your job application, no 23 _____ how well you think you can 24 _____ it up, for sooner of later you will be found out. So by all 25 _____ highlight the positives in your CV, but don't include blatant lies – even in the section on your leisure activities.

61

The Answer Key

A Business Parable: Consider the kind of people you work with
ANSWERS: 1-e / 2-c or d / 3-f or g / 4-j / 5-a / 6-h / 7-c or d / 8-f or g / 9-i / 10-b

A Business Parable: Who is watching you?
ANSWERS: 1-f / 2-b / 3-.i / 4-d / 5-c / 6-a / 7-k / 8-g / 9-e / 10-j / 11-h

Phrasal Nouns (i)
ANSWERS: 1 mark-up 2 blow-up 3 back-down 4 drop-off 5 letdown 6 sell-off 7 write-off 8 start-up 9 log-out 10 catch-up 11 put-down 12 wash-out

Phrasal Nouns (ii)
ANSWERS: 1 look-out 2 shake-up 3 outlay 4 breakdown 5 bail-out 6 upturn 7 setback 8 outcome 9 lay-offs 10 go-ahead 11 drawback 12 crackdown

Phrasal Nouns (iii)
ANSWERS: 1 feedback 2 changeover 3 come-on 4 run-around 5 cutbacks 6 put-on 7 cop-out 8 brush-off 9 lay-out 10 phase-out 11 mix-up 12 upkeep

Phrasal Adjectives
ANSWERS: 1 back-up 2 takeaway 3 stand-by 4 Carry-on 5 takeover 6 check-in 7 fallback 8 cooling-off 9 turnover 10 drop-out 11 warm-up 12 well-thought-out 13 trickle-down 14 breakaway 15 sought-after

How to write a Business Plan (word formation)
ANSWERS: 1 strategic 2 financial 3 summarising 4 overview 5 management 6 light 7 line 8 competitors 9 differentiates 10 personnel 11 operational 12 information 13 location 14 equipment 15 headcount 16 cashflow 17 reasonable 18 optimistic 19 accountant 20 slip-ups

Small Firms and the problem of Late Payments (word formation)
ANSWERS: 1 hardship 2 research 3 cashflow 4 overdrafts 5 resources 6 improving 7 ethics 8 fortune 9 real 10 likely 11 Notwithstanding 12 serve 13 alter 14 line 15 force 16 act 17 cover 18 usual 19 portion 20 reason

How to start working from home (word formation)
ANSWERS: 1 nightmare 2 commuter 3 gridlock 4 ability 5 whenever 6 equipment 7 depressing 8 factor 9 ensure 10 however 11 reliable 12 frustration 13 connection 14 recommendation 15 invaluable 16 introductory 17 hidden 18 agreement 19 deadline 20 subscription

Payment Fraud (word formation)
ANSWERS: 1 payment 2 con-artists 3 extremely 4 Innovation 4 automatically 6 speaking 7 consumers 8 software 9 passwords 10 careful 11 personal 12 information 13 Pickpockets 14 keypad 15 cashpoint 16 transaction 17 passwords 18 login 19 disclosing 20 unsolicited 21 website 22 Ensure 23 confirmation 24 fraudulently 25 reasonable

Irresponsible lending prohibited (word formation)
ANSWERS: 1 Lenders 2 mislead 3 repay 4 requirements 5 guidance 6 counteract 7 irresponsible 8 guidelines 9 enable 10 unscrupulous 11 creditworthiness 12 misleading 13 oppressive 14 behaviour 15 enforcing 16 agreement 17 reasonable 18 assessment 19 Additionally 20 commitments 21 misunderstanding 22 proce-

dures 23 ensuring 24 encouraged 25 unaffordable 26 unsustainable

A letter in application for a job
ANSWERS: 1-a /2-f / 3-a, b / 4-c / 5-c, d / 6-a, g / 7-b / 8-d / 9-b

A letter of Complaint
ANSWERS: 1-f / 2-a, b, c, g / 3-a / 4-c / 5-a, b, e / 6-b, c, d, e / 7-c, d, e / 8-b

A letter responding to a Complaint
ANSWERS: 1-a / 2-f / 3-a, d / 4-c, d / 5-a, c, d, e / 6-c / 7-b

A letter to find out more information about a product
ANSWERS: 1b / 2a / 3a or d / 4b or e / 5a or b / 6b / 7b or c / 8a or c or e / 9b or d / 10b / 11b or d (use b if the person is referred to by name at the start of the letter) 12 All three options would be inappropriate

Phrasal Verbs with INTO
ANSWERS: 1 turned 2 stepping 3 fell 4 look 5 ran 6 playing 7 eat 8 grew 9 buy 10 check 11 change 12 came 13 break 14 laid 15 hack

Phrasal Verbs with AWAY
ANSWERS: 1 get 2 giving 3 came 4 turned 5 plugging 6 go 7 drive 8 keep 9 soothe 10 bring 11 dreaming 12 put 13 backed 14 crept 15 frittering

Phrasal Verbs with OVER
ANSWERS: 1 get 2 look 3 win 4 came 5 think 6 stay 7 turned 8 standing 9 put 10 move 11 is 12 walk 13 take 14 carry 15 poring

Phrasal Verbs with OUT
ANSWERS: 1 figure 2 talk 3 pick 4 stick 5 block 6 brings 7 get 8 stamp 9 move 10 fly 11 find 12 fell 13 set 14 phase 15 make

Does money make you happy? (Use of the articles)
ANSWERS: 1 The 2 ___ 3 the 4 ___ 5 ___ 6 a 7 The 8 the 9 ___ 10 the 11 ___ 12 ___ 13 the 14 a 15 ___ 16 ___ 17 a 18 ___ 19 ___ 20 a 21 ___ 22 the 23 ___ 24 the 25 ___

The end of the cheque (use of the articles)
ANSWERS: 1 the 2 a 3 the 4 the 5 the 6 ___ 7 ___ 8 A 9 a 10 an 11 a 12 a 13 a 14 ___ 15 The 16 the 17 a 18 the 19 The 20 the 21 a 22 ___ 23 the 24 the 25 ___ 26 a 27 the 28 the 29 the 30 the 31 A 32 a 33 a 34 the 35 an

Verbs followed by the Gerund or the Infinitive
ANSWERS: 1-b / 2-a / 3-f / 4-c / 5-t / 6-n / 7-j / 8-s / 9-p / 10-d / 11-e / 12-l / 13-o / 14-k / 15-g / 16-q / 17-I /18-m / 19-r / 20-h

How to do well at Interviews (words confused and words misused)
ANSWERS: 1 managed 2 a position 3 suits 4 the 5 you can 6 should 7 to work / work 8 but 9 done 10 experience 11 achieve / to achieve 12 give 13 track 14 than 15 that / who 16 blank 17 asking 18 on 19 the 20 in mind

Built-in Obsolescence (words confused and words misused)
ANSWERS: 1 gets on my nerves 2 the 3 designed / made 4 last 5 computers 6 worse 7 if / when 8 the wind 9 cash 10 latest 11 discover / find out 12 The 13 the 14 continually 15 of 16 of 17 against 18 However 19 being 20 having 21 choice

Ethical Consumerism (words confused and words misused)
ANSWERS: 1 Money 2 go 3 we spend 4 save / to save 5 that / which 6 a price 7 down 8 clothes 9 that / which 10 petrol (British English) / gas (American English) 11 meanwhile 12 life 13 produce 14 human rights 15 into 16 consumers 17 However 18 the 19 favouring 20 as a whole

The causes of Inflation (words confused and words misused)
ANSWERS: 1 underlying 2 inflation 3 level 4 considering / looking at 5 as 6 However 7 alternatively 8 prepared / willing 9 proportion 10 rising 11 sustained 12 unless 13 the other 14 falls 15 as 16 cause 17 is an indication of / reflects 18 relative 19 tends 20 increase 21 overtime 22 hire 23 recruit 24 trade balance 25 in line with

Green banking or ethical banking - What's the difference?
ANSWERS: 1 choosing 2 a 3 preference / taste 4 which 5 conscientious 6 concerned 7 effect 8 prevent / stop 9 from saving 10 Banks 11 the money 12 common 13 in 14 the 15 principle 16 harm 17 wildlife 18 the 19 the money 20 the 21 However 22 said 23 neither 24 down to 25 conscience

Noun Phrases with Dependent Prepositions (i)
ANSWERS: 1-j / 2-f / 3-i / 4-h / 5-g / 6-a / 7-c / 8-h / 9-d / 10-e

1 have (no) doubts about 2 find a way of 3 have a flair for 4 in contact with 5 have access to / have an advantage over 6 take (so little) interest in 7 take comfort from 8 have (no) designs on 9 have a go at 10 having second thoughts over

Noun Phrases with Dependent Prepositions (ii)
ANSWERS: 1-a / 2-i / 3-f / 4-j / 5- e / 6-h / 7-g / 8-c / 9-d / 10-b

1 gain control over 2 have (no) knowledge of 3 have (every) confidence in 4 make allowances for 5 give (our full) support to 6 take courage from 7 in two minds about / have a (damaging) effect on 8 take a (long hard) look 9 gain an insight into

Noun Phrases with Dependent Prepositions (iii)
ANSWERS: 1-b / 2-c / 3-i / 4-g / 5-d / 6-j / 7/a / 8-h / 9-f / 10-e

1 have (no) regrets over 2 be of benefit to 3 take part in 4 take

advantage of 5 get (no) pleasure from 6 be an expert a 7 have (no) qualms about 8 feelings (we may) have towards 9 in the mood for 10 get a grip on

Adjectives with Dependent Prepositions (i)
ANSWERS: 1-h / 2-c / 3-i / 4-a / 5-b / 6-d / 7-f / 8-g / 9-j / 10-e

1 blamed for 2 hopeful of 3 obsessed with 4 committed to 5 exempt from 6 concerned about 7 tempted into 8 bemused over 9 depressed by 10 intent on

Adjectives with Dependent Prepositions (ii)
ANSWERS: 1-h / 2-i / 3-a / 4-j / 5-e / 6-b / 7-c / 8-g / 9-d / 10-f

1 annoyed over 2 renowned for 3 come close to 4 transformed into / proud of 5 content with 6 confused about 7 Inspired by 8 derived from 9 good at

Uncountable Nouns (i)
ANSWERS: 1-k / 2-g / 3-m / 4-c / 5-d / 6-i / 7-b / 8-a / 9-j / 10-e / 11-h / 12-l / 13-f

1 lack of confidence / cause for concern 2 form of slavery 3 show of support 4 call for peace 5 source of satisfaction 6 time of (global economic) uncertainty 7 campaign of violence 8 sense of calling 9 medium for (human) communication 10 sign of (your) discontent 11 wealth of information 12 bonds of trust

Uncountable Nouns (ii)
ANSWERS: 1-g / 2-e / 3-i / 4-b / 5-a / 6-f / 7-d / 8-j / 9-k / 10-h / 11-c

1 period of (economic) hardship 2 source of revenue 3 Table of Contents 4 programme of (continuous professional) development 5 sense of unease 6 form of barter 7 Lack of appreciation

8 array of information 9 case of (racial) discrimination 10 cause of (your job) stress 11 realm of uncertainty

What sort of manager are you?

Now add up your points and check your score. Give yourself 3 points for the answer *Most of the Time*, 2 points for *Sometimes*, and 1 point for *Never*.

If you have 31 to 36 points: Congratulations! You appear to have some very strong managerial skills. You communicate openly with your staff by sharing information and helping them feel secure in their roles. You recognize the importance of setting expectations, you avoid negative reinforcement, and you graciously acknowledge a job well done. Your respect for your team is evident, and it's very likely that they feel the same way about you.

If you have 25 to 30 points: Your managerial skills are on the way to being great, though you may be struggling a bit with communication. Remember that communication is a two way street - share your expectations, your appreciation and your knowledge. But don't be afraid to ask your staff to share their thoughts as well. You know the right things to do. Now you just have to commit to doing them all the time. As a manager, consistency is incredibly important.

If you have 19 to 24 points: It looks like you still have a little work to do. Treating your subordinates will little respect, using intimidation to get your way, or failing to provide positive feedback - *even sometimes* - can have a tremendous impact on employee morale. The good news is this: you can definitely make some simple changes that will have a big impact. Use the list above to help you focus on the areas you need help with. There are plenty of books, seminars and workshops out there aimed at helping you become the leader you know you can be.

If you have 12 to 18 points: Not everyone is meant for management, and you need to face the facts: you responded with "never" to the majority of the statements above. Look at these items. A strong leader should be doing each of these things "most of the time". Sure, it's not always easy. But being a leader is tough. You have to be willing to listen to others, acknowledge your own mistakes, and communicate in a respectful manner. Take a good long look at the list above and ask yourself if you can meet these standards. And if you can't (or aren't willing to) maybe it's time to reconsider what role you are best suited to.

Conditionals (i)
ANSWERS: 1 h / 2 l / 3 b / 4 c / 5 k / 6 j / 7 d / 8 i / 9 a / 10 f / 11 e / 12 g

Conditionals (ii)
ANSWERS: 1 e / 2 f / 3 j / 4 a / 5 g / 6 b / 7 i / 8 l / 9 c / 10 d / 11 h / 12 k

Being self-employed and how to punctuate it!
ANSWERS: a A comma is required after an IF clause in front position in a sentence b No comma is used when the IF clause comes second in a sentence c A comma is required before THOUGH d No comma is used before a defining clause e A comma is required before a non-defining clause f A comma is required after the connector HOWEVER in front position g A comma is required after the connector MOREOVER in front position h A comma is required after a participle clause I A comma is required after the sentence opener IN MY OPINION j No comma is used before BECAUSE

Connectors and Modifiers (i)
ANSWERS: 1 a / 2 k / 3 b / 4 i / 5 j / 6 l / 7 g / 8 d / 9 h / 10 c / 11 e / 12 f

Connectors and Modifiers (ii)
ANSWERS: 1 1 / 2 a / 3 i / 4 e / 5 d / 6 j / 7 k / 8 h / 9 b / 10 c / 11 f / 12 g

Proverbs about Work
ANSWERS: 1 h / 2 a / 3 d / 4 b / 5 j / 6 g / 7 i / 8 f / 9 k / 10 e / 11 c / 12 l

How Trustworthy are you?
Scoring: How many "always" did you have?

7-8: You are undoubtedly a trustworthy person, focused on building trust in your relationships.

5-7: Keep working at it. You will reap results by changing your behaviour and, at the same time, become more popular among your colleagues too.

Less than 5: Get busy before it's too late! Buy a self-help book to learn how to improve your trustworthiness or consider some kind of counselling or therapy to address the issues that are clearly causing you trouble at work.

How ethical are you at Work?
If you scored:

All A's — You're perfect and we should all be as pure as you! As long as you're not gloating about your ethical infallibility, you serve as a great role model for those around you

Mostly A's — You're not perfect, but no one is, so don't beat yourself up over it. Every now and then you stray, so just listen to the little voice that tells you to do the right thing most of the time a little more often

Mostly B's — You've forgotten a few things your parents taught you, but you could do worse – much worse – so all is not lost. Just think twice before you make a few decisions and you'll soon put things to right.

Mostly C's — Sometimes you teeter close the edge of unethical and might even be damaging your career as a result, but fortunately you can still redeem yourself now and then. And with a little hard work, you can probably perform some damage control and get back on the right track again.

All C's — Let's be honest, your reputation is probably not so great. In fact, people probably check their wallets once you've left to make sure nothing's stolen. Now's the time to decide if you want to turn over a new leaf and start afresh, with strong relationships and a better reputation ahead to look forward to as a result.

How satisfied are you with your job?
0-3: You have little to no satisfaction with your work. You may feel undervalued, or a job that was once challenging has now come to a standstill. Consider whether it's the job itself or the company that is making you unhappy and find a place or career that changes that.

4-6: You have some satisfaction with your job, whether it's the relationship you've developed with the people you work with or the work itself that you're doing. However, you may want to consider where this career is taking you and a change of direction might be what is required at this point in time.

7-9: Overall, you're satisfied with your job, but you may feel a little overwhelmed or stressed at times, and probably wish that you had more time to balance your work and personal life.

10-12: You are really satisfied with your job and while you look around once in a while to see what else is available, it's only because you want to consider your options, know your value, and keep your mind on where your career is heading.

13-15: Congratulations! You have a job that you find challenging in a company where you feel valued so make sure you hold on to it. Money isn't the sole driver of getting you out of bed in the morning, passion is, which is just how it should be.

Plural Nouns / Uncountable Nouns
ANSWERS: 1 consideration 2 savings / advice 3 jeans / trainers 4 guesswork 5 takings 6 rubbish 7 valuables 8 progress 9 earnings 10 harm 11 tidings 12 conditions 13 outgoings 14 accommodation / insurance / baggage 15 timing / room

Gerund or Infinitive
ANSWERS: 1-f / 2-b / 3-m / 4-j / 5-a / 6-k / 7-n / 8-l / 9-h / 10-g / 11-i / 12-o / 13-d / 14-e / 15-c

Verbs always followed by DOING consider / enjoy / imagine / keep / mind / resent / risk

Verbs always followed by TO DO agree / attempt / decide / hope / manage / offer / plan / resolve

Everything you always wanted to know about asking for a pay rise
ANSWERS 1-f 2-k 3-d 4-a 5-h 6-c 7-l 8-e 9-g 10-i 11-j 12-b

Everything you always wanted to know about going bankrupt
ANSWERS 1-d 2-c 3-j 4-g 5-f 6-e 7-i 8-b 9-a 10-h

One Word, Three Uses (i)
ANSWERS: Q1 street / Q2 stand / / Q3 give / Q4 clear / Q5 air / Q6 turn

One Word, Three Uses (ii)
ANSWERS: Q1 stock / Q2 clean / Q3 sound / Q4 home / Q5 call / Q6 pick

One Word, Three Uses (iii)
ANSWERS: Q1 open / Q2 check / Q3 leave / Q4 let / Q5 charge / Q6 do

S-Word Puzzle
ANSWERS: 1 salary 2 assure 3 resign 4 lesson 5 please 6 prices 7 crisis 8 insist 9 closes 10 resume 11 invest 12 stress

F-Word Puzzle
ANSWERS: 1 favour 2 offers 3 effort 4 profit 5 bereft 6 relief 7 belief 8 pacify 9 coffee 10 prefer 11 offend 12 freeze

UK water imports 'unsustainable'
ANSWERS: 1 worsening 2 shortages 3 unsustainable 4 footprint 5 critical 6 global 7 correspondingly 8 consumption 9 pressure 10 methodology 11 usage 12 responsible 13 remainder 14 considerate 15 caring 16 conservation 17 examine 18 exchange 19 electrical 20 consumption

R-Word Puzzle
ANSWERS: 1 recall 2 argued 3 borrow 4 regret 5 future 6 bother 7 matter 8 import 9 shares 10 spread 11 orders 12 rather

L-Word Puzzle
ANSWERS: 1 losers 2 allows 3 belief 4 follow 5 futile 6 retail 7 detail 8 settle 9 fallen 10 Unless 11 blames 12 longer

How to give an Effective Presentation

3. False. You should look at your audience. Eye contact is vital if you are to judge their understanding so that you can change the pace of your delivery if necessary.

4. False. Use notes instead. You should never, never read your speech from a sheet as it sends people off to sleep and suggests you lack mastery of your material.

6. False. The best approach is to vary the tone and level of your voice. This maintains interest. You should speak clearly and project your voice, rather than shouting. Talking quietly in key segments means that your listeners will need to actively listen to those parts of your presentation.

7. False Avoid excessive body movements and gestures whenever possible. Hand gestures can be used for emphasis only.

12. False. Confidence comes from practice. The more presentations you give, the better you will get at it. So don't give up and keep on trying.

What a person does for a living

ANSWERS: 1 life coach 2 civil servant 3 tree surgeon 4 customs officer 5 faith healer 6 spin doctor 7 fitness instructor 8 flight attendant 9 dental hygienist 10 general practitioner 11 traffic warden 12 interior decorator

How to produce the perfect CV

ANSWERS: 1 key / 2 laid / 3 assume / 4 hard / 5 regarded / 6 foot / 7 save / 8 whether / 9 present / 10 detract / 11 points / 12 sure / 13 comb / 14 plug / 15 justified / 16 perception / 17 mind / 18 end / 19 leave / 20 carry / 21 relevant / 22 embellish / 23 matter / 24 cover / 25 means

B O O K S

O is a symbol of the world, of oneness and unity. In different cultures it also means the "eye," symbolizing knowledge and insight. We aim to publish books that are accessible, constructive and that challenge accepted opinion, both that of academia and the "moral majority."

Our books are available in all good English language bookstores worldwide. If you don't see the book on the shelves ask the bookstore to order it for you, quoting the ISBN number and title. Alternatively you can order online (all major online retail sites carry our titles) or contact the distributor in the relevant country, listed on the copyright page.

See our website **www.o-books.net** for a full list of over 500 titles, growing by 100 a year.

And tune in to myspiritradio.com for our book review radio show, hosted by June-Elleni Laine, where you can listen to the authors discussing their books.

mySpiritRadio